Fan Oven Cooking Times and Temperatures

A Selection of Recipes for You to Enjoy

Bernice Hurst

D0620541

W. Foulsham & Co. Ltd.

London • New York • Toronto • Cape Town • Sydney

Colour Photography by Joe Windsor-Williams

W. FOULSHAM & COMPANY LIMITED
Yeovil Road, Slough, Berkshire, SLI 4JH
ISBN 0-572-01050-8

Printed in Spain by Cayfosa, Barcelona

CONTENTS

INTRODUCTION

Not so many years ago, buying an oven was a simple matter of choosing gas or electric and then deciding on the style which suited the kitchen. With today's options, the choice is far more difficult. The consumer needs to be more knowledgeable about cooking appliances and their capabilities than ever before. What, for instance, is the difference between a British and a Continental oven? What is a fan oven, a fan-assisted oven, a convection oven, a multifunction oven, a combination oven? What is turbo-grilling, thermo-grilling, hot air grilling, high speed or accelerated cooking? Each manufacturer has its own names for the functions its ovens can perform. How similar, or different, are these functions?

More complicated still, once you have made a choice, how do you use the oven? Is it really different and if so, in what way? As with other domestic appliances, some ovens offer far more options than you are likely to use every day. How can you make the best use of them? Modern ovens can offer up to ten or eleven programmes. What are they, why do you need them and how do you use them?

Whether you need help to choose an oven or to use it, the purpose of this book is to answer questions about the various facilities modern ovens offer. The recipes will supplement your favourite cookbooks, giving you new ideas, but also will offer comparisons for the various cooking methods. Each recipe gives conventional oven cooking times and temperatures so that you can cook in this way but also to offer instant comparisons if you are adapting to a fan or multifunction oven. It also gives the fan cooking times and temperatures and recommendations for the best options to use if you have a multifunction oven.

Fan, multifunction and combination ovens can save time and energy if you know how to use them. They are not as complicated as they may initially appear, and we hope that by the time you have read this book you will be wholeheartedly convinced of their advantages.

Lamb with Chickpeas and Apricots (page 58)

Fan Ovens

The term 'fan oven' is generic, and is applied to any oven which contains a fan element. Many manufacturers use trade names, often created exclusively for their own use, to differentiate their own ovens from everyone else's. Although each brand contains certain individual features, and not every model offers the same combination of options, there are some things which they all, as fan ovens, have in common.

The confusion arises when manufacturers refer to convection, hot air and fan-assisted ovens. Ovens containing fans are often called by these somewhat unclear and inaccurate names. Although all ovens are technically convection ovens, the title itself generally refers to forced convection or fan ovens, as opposed to conventional ovens which use natural convection. Similarly, fan ovens are often described as hot air ovens, a reference to the fact that the fan circulates hot air. A fan-assisted convection oven is just what its name indicates, an oven in which the fan assists the convection heat which cooks the food. The jargon and terminology can be misleading — if you are confused, make sure you ask.

Natural Convection

All ovens operate by convection, that is the transmission of heat from the oven's elements through the food being cooked. Conventional, traditional ovens operate by natural convection, with the heat rising upwards through currents. In British ovens, the heating elements are usually placed on the two side walls of the oven. In Continental ovens, the elements are situated on the floor and ceiling. Wherever the elements are located, however, hot air rises so that the bottom of the oven is always cooler than the top. This is why pans must be rotated when baking to ensure even results. It is also the reason why roast dinners, for example, can be cooked successfully, with the meat in the lower, cooler part of the oven so that it can be cooked slowly and the Yorkshire pudding in the upper, hotter part of the oven so that it can be cooked more quickly. Shelf position is very important in conventional convection ovens — depending on the results you want, you choose which part of the oven to use.

Forced Convection

Fan ovens operate through forced convection. A fan is positioned behind the back wall of the oven and draws in air which is heated by an element around the fan. The air is then forced back into the oven chamber via ducts in the wall. The constant circulation of hot air, released into the oven at several different points, ensures that the temperature is the same throughout the oven. It also means that the heat surrounds the food being cooked rather than being directed at it from above, below or to one side. The implications and advantages of this are explained on page 11.

A fan-assisted oven uses the fan to circulate heat which comes from another source, that is the elements situated at the top, bottom or sides of the oven. Multifunction ovens, which will be described in more detail later, operate in this way as well as acting as both fan and conventional ovens.

Multifunction Ovens

Multifunction ovens contain heating elements in the floor and ceiling of the oven, as well as having a fan element. They can be operated in several different combinations:

conventional top and bottom elements only
fan element only
fan circulating heat from either the top or bottom element
fan circulating heat from both the top and bottom elements (only available in some models)
top element (grill) (broiler) or bottom element only

In addition, many multifunction ovens have a programme whereby the fan operates without any heating element, circulating cool air only to speed defrosting time or to slightly thaw delicate frozen foods such as sorbets and cream cakes. Note: this is not the same as defrosting with a microwave!

The choice of functions enables you to cook different dishes, or meals, in any way you prefer. For batch baking and quick cooking, the fan is best. For slower cooking, or when you prefer to have variable temperatures in the different parts of the oven, you can choose to cook conventionally. The advantages of using the fan to circulate heat from the top or bottom of the oven are discussed in detail on page 14. Incorporating the grill element in the oven chamber saves space by eliminating the need for a separate eye-level grill or second, smaller oven unit. Food can generally be grilled with the door closed, a further way to save energy.

It is quite likely that you will feel most comfortable with just two or three of the options available on a multifunction oven, using them for most of your everyday cooking. But the capability is there when you choose to use it, offering a freedom and variety that is as convenient as it is new.

Combination Ovens

These are the newest innovation in the oven market, combining either a conventional, fan or multifunction oven with a microwave oven in a single unit. Their most obvious advantage is that they combine the speed of a microwave with the browning and crisping capability of a conventional or fan oven. The microwave can be operated on its own or in combination with the oven's other functions, giving unlimited choices of cooking methods.

For all the help microwave ovens offer the cook, they are generally most suitable for use as supplementary ovens. Cakes often come out steamed rather than baked, pastry does not have the crisp, flaky texture we generally prefer, and artificial colourings or special browning dishes have to be used to give a golden brown appearance. Because of the things they can't do, they are not replacements and cannot be used to the exclusion of a conventional oven.

Combination ovens offer the best features of the microwave and the conventional (or the fan) oven at the same time. You can use the microwave function on its own to do any or all of the things a microwave does to perfection or you can use the conventional or fan oven on its own for any of the jobs which only they can do properly. Some manufacturers offer a multifunction oven with a microwave capability, resulting in the maximum number of cooking combinations.

But the beauty of a combination oven is the fact that the microwave and conventional or fan functions can be used simultaneously. Some models can also be programmed to automatically alternate the microwave and conventional or fan functions. You can thus switch, either manually or automatically, from one cooking method to another to take advantage of the ultimate in high technology. You can roast or bake in record time with the texture, flavour and appearance you would expect with traditional cooking methods. You can also cook from frozen, with no worries about soggy, cardboard-textured pastry or pale, unattractive roasts or cakes. In many models you can even use metal or tin foil dishes, generally not suitable for ordinary microwaves.

Strawberry Shortcake (page 98)

MULTIFUNCTION COOKING: THE OPTIONS

Conventional (Natural Convection) Cooking

With all the benefits that fan, multifunction, microwave and combination ovens have to offer, why would anyone still choose to cook conventionally? There are two answers. The first is that there are times when you want to use your oven for cooking several dishes simultaneously but on slightly different temperatures. Because the heat rises in a conventional oven, the higher shelf positions are hotter than the lower ones. So it is possible, for instance, to braise your vegetables or cook a casserole on a low shelf while baking potatoes or finishing off a dessert on a higher shelf. In some models, plates and serving dishes can be warmed on the floor of the oven while the meal is cooking.

Secondly, fan and microwave ovens cook food quickly. You may not always find this an advantage, preferring to braise casseroles or bake puddings slowly and gently. Or you may prefer the results when delicate soufflés, sponges or rich fruit cakes are cooked conventionally. Crusts on baked goods often come out browner and crisper when cooked in a conventional oven. You will have to be guided by personal taste when deciding how to cook various dishes — if you like soft crusts, for instance, use the fan oven.

There are things to watch out for in a conventional oven, however. Best results are achieved when cooking on one shelf only. If you are using more than one shelf, tins will probably need to be rotated halfway through the cooking time. Unless a recipe indicates otherwise, use the middle shelf of the oven when cooking on one level only. Pre-heating a conventional oven can take up to 15 or 20 minutes.

Fan (Convection or Hot Air) Cooking

There are so many good reasons for cooking with a fan oven

that it is simplest to list them all first and then explain them in detail.

1. Heat is intensive therefore cooking times and temperatures are generally lower.
2. Pre-heating is not always necessary; when it is, as for baking, fan ovens do not take as long as conventional ovens to reach the required temperature.
3. Time and energy savings, plus the ability to fill the oven to maximum capacity, achieve considerable cost savings.
4. Even temperatures throughout the oven make it ideal for batch baking.
5. Circulating heat seals meat and creates a rotisserie effect.
6. Circulating heat prevents tastes and smells mingling.

The circulating air in a fan oven is very intense, ensuring that the heat penetrates the food more rapidly than in a conventional oven. This means that the food will cook faster. Dishes taking more than one hour to cook generally need ten minutes per hour less than they would in a conventional oven. Dishes needing less than an hour might be ready a few minutes sooner, but this is something you will soon learn to judge from experience.

Rapid heat transfer also means that the temperature in a fan oven need not be as high as in a conventional oven. As a general rule, most manufacturers recommend setting the oven approximately 10–20°C lower than you would normally. Although you may find that your own oven needs to be adjusted slightly more or less than this, it is a fairly accurate guideline. Some fan ovens have a lower range of temperatures than do conventional ovens, as the highest settings are unnecessary. The hotter the oven in some cases, the wider the variation. For instance, if you are used to cooking at 180°C you would reduce the temperature by 15–20°C. But if you are cooking at 225°C, you might have to reduce the temperature by 25–30°C. So you may find that your oven's thermostat only goes up to 200°C but will still be equivalent to the higher settings that you have used in the past. It is always best to follow the instruction booklet supplied by the manufacturer until you are used to your oven and can make your own allowances.

Time/Energy Savings

As soon as a fan oven is switched on, the fan begins to draw in the air and heat it. Most food, therefore, will start cooking immediately. Pre-heating is only necessary when you are baking soufflés, fatless sponges, yeast mixtures or scones. Even then, because the heat from the fan is so intense, the required temperature will be reached in just 5 minutes, considerably less than with a conventional oven.

Because the temperature is uniform throughout the oven chamber, there is no problem about filling the oven to its maximum capacity. Whether you are batch baking or cooking an entire meal, every inch of shelf space can be used to achieve even results. The oven will therefore be switched on for a shorter period — you can cook the starter, main course and dessert simultaneously rather than wait for one dish to finish cooking before starting on the next.

To summarise, there are several reasons why cooking with a fan oven will save you both time and energy: shorter pre-heating and cooking times, lower temperature settings and the ability to use the oven to its fullest capacity. These savings generate cost savings, making a fan oven extremely economical to use.

Getting the Most from Your Oven

Batch baking is one of the jobs for which a fan oven is perfect. Provided that you leave enough room for the air to circulate around the baking pans, the even temperature throughout the oven will ensure that you get the same results whichever shelf you use. The large pans provided with your oven should not be used when batch baking however if they fit directly on to the side walls of the oven as they will not let the air circulate properly. You must leave clearance space on all sides. Use your own baking trays or cake tins on the oven's wire shelves to get the best results possible.

Similarly, if you are preparing several dishes at once on different shelves, never place anything under one of the baking trays provided. Always use the wire shelves and casseroles or baking dishes which leave clearance space around them. Consult your instruction book for more exact information on shelf positions. If the oven is very full, you may have to allow a few extra minutes' cooking time, but this is another matter which will vary slightly and must be judged from experience. Food placed near the back of the oven may also brown faster than food at the front because of the heat coming from the fan, so check to see if pans need to be turned. If cooking on one level only, use the centre shelf position unless the recipe indicates otherwise. If using more than one shelf, try to stagger the pans if possible so that they aren't directly above or below each other.

By circulating the air around the food and sealing it on all sides, fan ovens can be used for grilling (broiling) as well as roasting. Chops, fish, steaks, hamburgers, kebabs and other dishes can be cooked in the fan oven and taste as if they came from a rotisserie. Nor do they need to be turned over halfway to ensure even browning. Chickens and roasts do not need to be basted. Simply place the food on the wire rack with a roasting pan underneath to catch any drips and it will be thoroughly cooked without needing to be turned. If you want to grill on several shelves simultaneously, place the roasting pan on the floor of the oven and the food directly on the wire shelves.

Pre-heating is not usually necessary and the lower temperatures needed when using the fan oven mean that there will be less spitting and hence less cleaning up to do. Some manufacturers also offer an automatic probe for using with roasts. The probe is inserted into the oven wall at one end, the meat at the other, and measures the internal temperature of the meat. You programme both the meat temperature and the oven temperature you want. An automatic timer will let you know when the meat is cooked. In some models, the fan and grill work alternately when roasting, offering an additional guarantee that the surface will be crisp while the centre remains moist and succulent.

There is one more important bonus. When the fan draws the air in and re-circulates it, it prevents smells and flavours from mingling. This means that your lemon meringue pie will not taste of fish, for instance, and you can cook an entire meal all at once. Suggestions for various combinations of dishes which can be cooked at the same temperature settings are given on page 28.

Traditional Grilling

There are times when traditional grilling (broiling) is more convenient or suitable than grilling with the fan. Toast, gratin dishes which just need quick surface browning, bacon rashers and thin cuts of meat, for example, all benefit from the direct heat of a radiant or infra-red grill. Many ovens also offer the option of cooking with half of the grill only, ideal for small portions. Whether the door should remain open or closed varies, and you must consult your instruction book to be certain.

If you have a microwave oven, a traditional grill can be used to finish off dishes which need to be browned after cooking. Meringue toppings for desserts and grated cheese for savoury meals can also be flashed under the grill until they are golden.

Grill with Fan

Most manufacturers have got their own name for this function which is basically grilling (broiling) on indirect rather than direct heat. The fan circulates heat coming from above the food, sealing it on all sides and generally eliminating the need for turning. It produces a result similar to that of a rotisserie, crisp on the outside, but juicy on the inside.

All the advantages of circulating air and cooking with a fan oven in general are supplemented by the direct heat coming from above the food to provide extra browning. For dishes where a golden topping is important, the fan circulates the heat to cook the whole dish, while the grill makes the surface crisp and brown. It is most suitable for use with small cuts of meat, fish or gratin dishes.

Some manufacturers offer a slightly different feature to create this effect. The grill and fan operate alternately, making the function suitable for larger joints of meat, although they should be turned halfway through the cooking time to ensure that they are thoroughly browned on all sides.

Bottom Element with Fan

This function is often referred to as the pâtissière's or baker's programme as it is especially suitable for pastry baking. The fan circulates heat coming from below the food, ensuring that the base is thoroughly cooked as well as the inside. Single crust pies and quiches benefit particularly from being cooked in this way — the fan cooks the filling, while the heat coming from the bottom of the oven makes the pastry shell crisp and brown.

In some models it is possible to use the bottom element only, without the fan, a method recommended by the manufacturers for making preserves. The bottom element can also be used to finish off pizzas or other pies to ensure that the base is completely cooked and crisp.

Defrosting

Although defrosting in the fan oven isn't as fast as defrosting in a microwave oven, it is faster than leaving food at room temperature. Not all ovens have this facility, but those which do use the fan to circulate the air without heating it. This can reduce defrosting time by approximately one third of the time needed if the food is left on the kitchen table. The gentle circulation of air is also useful for softening ice cream, sorbets, frozen fruit or cream cakes and for proving bread.

Combination Ovens

Combination ovens dispel the shortcomings of microwave ovens and can, in some households, replace traditional ovens entirely. They are simple to use once you have the knack, but are the most complicated in terms of adapting your favourite recipes. Because of the varying features from one brand to another, it is difficult to give hard and fast rules for conversion. For instance, some combination ovens have fans, some have top and bottom elements or grill (broiler) elements only, and some have all these options. When using the combination feature, the microwave can operate either alternately or simultaneously with the oven's other functions depending on the model you have purchased. Furthermore, the degree to which temperatures and the proportions of microwave time to conventional or fan cooking time are pre-set varies. When selecting a combination oven, you must decide how much flexibility you want — do you want the oven to think for you, or would you prefer to choose the temperatures and combinations of microwave and conventional times for each dish as you cook it?

Cooking in a combination oven is usually described as accelerated or high-speed. This is true, but in addition to its advantages it does create a few problems. In order to brown food in a short cooking time, high oven temperatures are necessary. Therefore the oven itself gets hotter than a microwave would and splashing makes careful cleaning necessary. Most manufacturers solve this problem by using catalytic or pyrolitic linings, but grill elements and doors must be kept immaculate for best results.

The high temperatures necessary also nullify the economy of standard microwaves to a certain extent — you use more power, therefore the cost of using the oven is somewhat higher. This only applies to the combination programme itself and the actual time savings can be as much as 25–50%, so costs can balance out in the long run.

Most combination ovens are larger internally than microwave ovens and will take large joints as well as being able to cope with several dishes at once. Turntables are generally available for the microwave-only function and can be switched off or removed when using the combination function. Shelves are often provided which further increase the oven's capacity.

Although pre-heating is usually unnecessary, there are exceptions as for puff pastry or Yorkshire pudding. The time needed is minimal however. With regard to cooking dishes, many combination ovens can take foil or metal dishes, but you must check your instruction manual for this. The higher temperatures used in combination cooking can damage special microwave dishes and again you must either check carefully or learn through trial and error which brands are suitable. Roast-in bags and deep dishes eliminate many of the spitting and cleaning problems. Clear or coloured glass dishes, heat resistant ceramic or china are generally the best to use for combination cooking. On the microwave, conventional or fan programmes you can use the same pans you would normally.

The most important benefit of combination cooking is its ability to combine a microwave's speed with the taste, texture and appearance of more traditional cooking methods. The microwave function on its own is best for any dish that is boiled or steamed, such as vegetables, fish, puddings, soups or sauces, for defrosting and reheating, for jam-making and small portions. The grill (broiler), conventional or fan function on its own is best for small items, particularly baked dishes such as biscuits or scones, individual steaks, chops, chicken pieces or kebabs or any dish which just needs quick browning. The combination function is superb for everything else. It can be used for roasts, pastry, cakes, frozen food which needs to be crisped and/or browned before serving, bread and anything which needs to be baked but looks most attractive with a golden finish. Pre-cooking can also be reduced or eliminated. Much of the preparation needed can be done on the microwave function (for example, melting butter or chocolate, preparing sauces, softening vegetables etc.) and the assembled dish then cooked on the fan,

conventional, grill or combination function as you prefer.
Those combination ovens which are also multifunction ovens,
incorporating the various options of fan plus top or bottom
elements as well as the microwave facility, offer even more
permutations.

Chicken with Thyme (page 74)

Fan, multifunction and combination ovens can offer up to ten or eleven operations within a single oven. Although the terminology differs from one manufacturer to another and individual models offer varying permutations, the basic choices available are shown below.

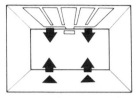

conventional oven (natural convection) cooking i.e. using the top and bottom elements of a standard electric oven

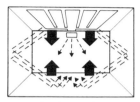

conventional oven plus microwave

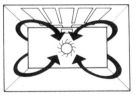

fan (forced convection) oven cooking

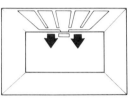

grilling using full or half power

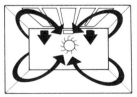

fan plus top element only i.e. grill (broiler)

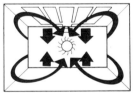

fan plus conventional oven i.e. fan plus heating from top and bottom elements

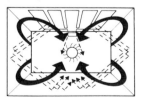

fan plus microwave

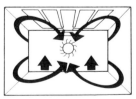

fan plus bottom element only

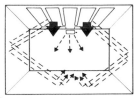

grill plus microwave

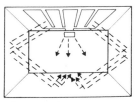

microwave alone

Multifunction Cooking — at a Glance

Conventional Cooking

The heat in a conventional or natural convection oven is generated from elements either in the top and bottom of the oven or behind the side walls. The heat rises, making the higher shelves hotter than the bottom shelves, enabling you to cook several dishes at varying temperatures simultaneously.

Conventional ovens can be used for all types of cooking but are most suitable for rich fruit cakes, yeast mixtures and soufflés or sponges with a high egg content. Bread and cakes cooked conventionally usually have a darker, crisper crust than those cooked in a fan oven.

Pans should be placed on the central shelf positions for best results unless you are cooking several dishes simultaneously and prefer to have one on a higher temperature than the other.

Fan Cooking

The heat in a fan, fan-assisted or forced convection oven is circulated by a fan situated behind the back wall of the oven, ensuring that the temperature is uniform on all shelves. The fan also prevents flavours and smells from mingling. Fan ovens need little or no preheating time, and cook on lower temperatures than conventional ovens. They are also faster than conventional ovens and can therefore save both time and energy. Fan ovens are suitable for all types of cooking and achieve superb results when batch baking.

Because the food is sealed on all sides at once, fan ovens can be used instead of traditional infra-red or radiant grills. There is no need to turn or baste during cooking.

Tins should be placed on the central shelf positions for best results. If you are batch baking, try to stagger the tins if possible.

Fan + Grill

Heat generated from the top, or grill element, of the oven is circulated by the fan with this setting. The result is that food is cooked from above and around simultaneously, allowing it to cook in its own juices while guaranteeing a golden topping.

Tins should be placed on the highest shelf position for best results.

Fan + Bottom

Heat generated from the bottom element, beneath the floor of the oven, is circulated by the fan with this setting. It is particularly useful for pastry baking, ensuring that both the base and the filling are thoroughly cooked.

Tins should be placed on the lowest shelf position for best results.

Grill only

All ovens, whether conventional or fan, will offer the option of using an infra-red or radiant grill positioned on the ceiling of the oven. In some cases you can use half of the grill only for small portions. Grills should be used with the oven door open unless the manufacturer specifies otherwise. Small portions of meat or fish, beefburgers, sausages and dishes needing quick surface browning only are best when cooked in a traditional grill.

As the heat is directed on to the food from above, the highest shelf position should be used for best results.

Defrost

On this setting the fan operates without any heat source, circulating cool air to gently defrost sorbets and ice cream, fresh cream desserts and soft fruit. It can also cut normal defrosting by up to one third of the usual time.

Not all models offer this facility, so check your instruction booklet carefully.

CONVERSION TABLES

Liquid Measurements

As conversions cannot always be exact, we recommend that you follow one set of measurements only.

Metric	Imperial	American
5 ml	1 tsp	1 tsp
15 ml	1 tbsp	1 tbsp
25–30 ml	1 fl oz	1 oz
50–60 ml	2 fl oz	¼ cup
225 ml	8 fl oz	1 cup (½ pint)
300 ml	½ pint	1 ¼ cups
450 ml	¾ pint	1 pt
575 ml	1 pint	2 ½ cups
1 litre	1 ¾ pints	4 ½ cups

Raisin Cheesecake (page 119)

Dry Measurements

As conversions cannot always be exact, we recommend that you follow one set of measurements only.

Metric	Imperial	American
5 ml	1 tsp	1 tsp
15 ml	1 tbsp	1 tbsp
110–125 g	4 oz	1/4 lb
225–250 g	8 oz	1/2 lb
450 g	1 lb	1 lb
1 kg	2.2 lb	2.2 lb

HOW TO COOK YOUR FAVOURITE DISHES

Cooking with a fan or multifunction oven is straightforward and very simple, but you must remember that it will cook faster than a conventional oven and require a lower temperature setting. To ensure that you can cook your favourite dishes without difficulty, the following conversions offer a few basic guidelines. If something doesn't appear in the table, the best rule is to set the oven 10–20°C lower than you would normally and to reduce cooking time by approximately 10 minutes per hour for dishes requiring more than 1 hour total cooking time. If your total cooking time is less than 1 hour, it will be approximately the same as usual. If you remember that each oven is as individual as the cook using it, however, you will soon be able to judge the variations for yourself.

	Fan oven temperature (°C)	Cooking time
Bread (450 g/1 lb loaf)	210°	30 minutes
Rolls	210°	20 minutes
Herb/Garlic Bread	200°	10 minutes
Scones (Biscuits)	200°	10 minutes
Biscuits or Cookies	175°	8–10 minutes
Shortbread	160°	25 minutes
Victoria Sponge or Plain Cake	160°	25 minutes
Swiss Roll (Jelly Roll)	210°	10 minutes
Fairy Cakes (Cupcakes)	180°	15 minutes
Rich Fruit Cake	130°	2½–3 hours
Individual Meringues	100°	3 hours

Meringue Layers (Pavlova)	130°	30 minutes
Meringue Topping for Pies	190°	7–8 minutes
Pastry (Baked Blind)	190°	15 minutes
Fruit Pies	170°	40 minutes
Choux Pastry	210°	15 minutes
Quiche or Open Tarts	180°	35–40 minutes
Fruit Compote	140°	45 minutes
Rice Pudding	140°	1½ hours
Baked Custard	170°	50 minutes
Bread and Butter Pudding	160°	30–40 minutes
Fruit Crumble	160°	45 minutes
Dessert Soufflés	170°	30 minutes
Shepherd's or Cottage Pie	180°	30 minutes
Fish Pie	160°	35 minutes
Casseroles (Meat)	160°	1½ hours
Casseroles (Poultry)	160°	1¼ hours
Baked Chops	160°	35 minutes
Baked Chicken Pieces	190°	30 minutes
Baked Fish, Whole (450g/1lb)	180°	30 minutes
Baked Fish, Fillets or Steaks	170°	20 minutes
Cannelloni or Lasagne	190°	30 minutes
Yorkshire Pudding (Large)	160°	45 minutes
Yorkshire Pudding (Individual) or Popovers	160°	30 minutes
Roast Potatoes	160°	1 hour
Baked Potatoes	190°	45 minutes
Crispy Jacket Potatoes	160°	1¼ hours
Macaroni Cheese	210°	20 minutes
Cheese Soufflé	170°	35 minutes
Stuffed Peppers	180°	30 minutes
Stuffed Tomatoes	175°	15 minutes
Braised Carrots or Brussels Sprouts	160°	45 minutes

ROASTING AND GRILLING GUIDELINES

Roasting

Food roasted in the fan oven has a crisp, crackly skin and moist, succulent flesh. Meat and fish are sealed on all sides simultaneously, eliminating the need for basting and turning.

Place the meat or fish on a wire rack with a roasting pan beneath it to catch the drippings and juice. Potatoes, onions and/or parsnips can be arranged in the pan to cook in the juices. Use the central shelf position in the oven or, if cooking a Yorkshire pudding, vegetables or dessert, place the roast on the second runner from the bottom and any other pans above rather than below. There is no need to preheat the oven when using it for roasting.

Some multifunction ovens offer the option of automatic roasting, whereby the grill (broiler) and fan operate alternately. In this instance the food does need to be turned halfway through cooking time so that it browns evenly.

	Fan oven temperature (°C)	Cooking time
Beef (on the bone)		
rare	175°	15 mins per 450 g/1 lb +25 mins
medium	175°	20 mins per 450 g/1 lb +25 mins
well done	175°	25 mins per 450 g/1 lb +25 mins
Beef (off the bone) rare	175°	20 mins per 450 g/1 lb +10 mins
medium	175°	20 mins per 450 g/1 lb +20 mins

	Fan oven temperature (°C)	Cooking time
well done	175°	25 mins per 450 g/1 lb +15 mins
Lamb (on the bone)	175°	20 mins per 450 g/1 lb +20 mins
Lamb (off the bone)	175°	25 mins per 450 g/1 lb +25 mins
Pork (on the bone)	190°	25 mins per 450 g/1 lb +25 mins
Pork (off the bone)	190°	35 mins per 450 g/1 lb +35 mins
Chicken	175°	20 mins per 450 g/1 lb +15 mins
Duck	175°	25 mins per 450 g/1 lb +15 mins
Turkey, stuffed (4 ½ kg/ 10 lb)	175°	3 hours
Turkey, unstuffed (4 ½ kg/10 lb)	175°	2 ½ hours

Grilling

Grilling (broiling) with the fan oven is more suitable for cooking large quantities than using the infra-red or radiant grill supplied with your oven. The rapid transfer of heat ensures that the food is sealed on all sides and that temperatures are even throughout the oven. Nor does the food need to be turned as the fan browns on all sides at once.

Place meat or fish to be grilled on the wire rack supplied with a drip pan or roasting pan beneath it. Tomatoes or mushrooms can be placed in the roasting pan to cook in the drippings from the meat or fish.

When grilling on several shelves simultaneously, place the roasting pan on the floor of the oven and the meat or fish to be grilled directly on the wire shelves.

Use the central shelf position when using one shelf only, or the second and third or second, third and fourth positions if using two or three shelves simultaneously.

For best results the oven should be preheated for 5 minutes before grilling. If fatty meats create smoke, reduce the temperature slightly but increase the cooking time as necessary.

	Fan oven temperature (°C)	*Cooking time*
Hamburgers (225 g/8 oz)		
rare	190°	10 minutes
medium	190°	15 minutes
well done	190°	20 minutes
Rump, fillet or sirloin steak (225 g/8 oz)		
rare	220°	10 minutes
medium	220°	12 minutes
well done	220°	15 minutes
T-bone steak		
rare	220°	15 minutes
medium	220°	20 minutes
well done	220°	25 minutes
Pork chops	200°	10–15 minutes
Lamb chops	200°	10–15 minutes
Whole fish (450 g/1 lb)	220°	15 minutes
Toasted sandwiches	200°	10–15 minutes
Sausages	200°	10–15 minutes

MENU SUGGESTIONS

Because smells and flavours do not mingle in a fan oven, it is possible to cook an entire meal at once, thereby using the oven to its full capacity. In addition to being very convenient, you can save both time and energy by taking advantage of this facility. Dishes with varying cooking times but similar temperatures can be selected and simply placed in the oven at the necessary intervals.

Alternatively, dishes which need similar cooking times can be prepared in advance and left to cook automatically by setting the oven's timer and leaving the meal to cook itself. There are a few provisos to remember when using the automatic timer, however. Food should not be left in the oven for more than 8 hours before cooking begins. Stuffed poultry should not be left for more than 1–2 hours maximum. Nor is it advisable to leave food in the oven for any length of time in warm weather. When cooking time is complete, the oven will switch off automatically. Although the oven will take some time to cool down, if you want to serve a hot meal you should plan your timetable accordingly.

The menus suggested below offer a few possibilities for whole meals to be cooked in your fan oven. Once you have got the knack of choosing dishes which need similar times and temperatures you will find just how helpful a fan oven can be when planning both family and dinner party meals.

	Fan oven temperature (°C)	Cooking time
Braised breast of veal	160°	1 ½ hours
New potatoes	160°	1 ½ hours
Glazed carrots	160°	1 ½ hours
Lemon layer pudding	160°	½ hour

Scrub 450 g/1 lb potatoes and arrange in a covered casserole with 50 g/2 oz/4 tbsp butter and 30 ml/2 tbsp water.

Mix 450 g/1 lb peeled and sliced carrots with 60 ml/4 tbsp butter and 5 ml/1 tsp golden (corn) syrup in a covered casserole.

Prepare the veal according to the recipe on page 71. Place on the bottom shelf of the oven and the casseroles on the third shelf from the bottom. Prepare the Lemon layer pudding according to the recipe on page 99. Put the pudding on the second shelf from the bottom of the oven when the veál comes out if you want to serve it hot. To serve the pudding cold, put it on the same shelf as the vegetables for the first ½ hour of the total cooking time and then remove to cool while the rest of the meal cooks.

Braised Breast of Veal (page 71), Lemon Layer Pudding (page 99)

	Fan oven temperature (°C)	Cooking time
Macaroni cheese	170°	35 minutes
Baked tomatoes	170°	35 minutes
Apple strudel	170°	35 minutes

Prepare the macaroni cheese according to your favourite recipe.

Cut a slice off the tops of 4 tomatoes and carefully scoop out the seeds. Toss a finely chopped clove of garlic, 5 ml/1 tsp chopped herbs and 30 ml/2 tbsp breadcrumbs in 30 ml/2 tbsp melted butter. Fill the tomatoes and arrange in an ovenproof dish. Drizzle with olive oil.

Prepare the apple strudel according to the recipe on page 107. Place the strudel on the second shelf from the bottom of the oven. Place the macaroni and tomatoes on the fourth shelf from the bottom. Leave the strudel to cool slightly while you serve the rest of the meal then sprinkle with sieved icing (confectioners') sugar. Pass a jug of cream separately.

	Fan oven temperature (°C)	Cooking time
Roast pork (1 ½ kg/3 ½ lb)	170°	1 ½ hours
Potato soufflé	170°	½ hour
Braised red cabbage	170°	½ hour
Apple pie or fruit crumble	170°	¾ hour

Prepare the pork in your favourite way. Place on a wire rack over a roasting pan and place on the bottom runner of the oven.

Prepare the potato soufflé and red cabbage according to the recipes on pages 57 and 54.

Put the soufflé, cabbage and pie or crumble into the oven ½ hour after the pork has started cooking. The dessert will then have a few minutes to cool down before serving at the end of the meal. The potatoes and cabbage should be placed on the third shelf from the bottom of the oven and the pie or crumble on the fourth shelf from the bottom.

	Fan oven temperature (°C)	Cooking time
Turkey breast en croûte	180°	35 minutes
Scalloped potatoes	180°	35 minutes
Petits pois or cauliflower		
Plum compote	180°	35 minutes

Prepare the turkey breast en croûte according to the recipe on page 79.

Peel and thinly slice 450 g/1 lb potatoes and arrange in layers in an ovenproof dish. Sprinkle each layer with salt, pepper and finely chopped onion and garlic. Dot the top layer with butter and pour over 150 ml/5 fl oz/⅔ cup milk or single (light) cream.

Wash 450 g/1 lb plums and place in an ovenproof dish with 30 ml/2 tbsp sugar, a cinnamon stick and 150 ml/5 fl oz/ ⅔ cup water. Cover the dish.

Place the turkey on the second shelf from the bottom of the oven. Place the potatoes and plums on the fourth shelf from the bottom. Serve with petits pois or cauliflower prepared in your favourite way.

	Fan oven temperature (°C)	Cooking time
Jacket potatoes	180°	1 hour
Cheese or Hot pepper soufflé	180°	35 minutes
Braised broccoli	180°	35 minutes
Baked bananas or pineapple	180°	15 minutes

Wash the potatoes well and prick with a fork to let the steam out. Place on the bottom shelf of the oven.

Prepare the cheese soufflé according to your favourite recipe or the hot pepper soufflé as on page 46.

Place 450 g/1 lb frozen broccoli in an ovenproof casserole with 30 ml/2 tbsp water. Cover tightly.

Prepare the bananas or pineapple according to the recipe on page 95.

Place the broccoli on the bottom shelf of the oven, along with the potatoes. Place the soufflé on the third shelf from the bottom of the oven. Place the bananas or pineapple on the centre shelf of the oven when you have removed the rest of the meal. Serve the fruit hot, accompanied by fresh cream or ice cream.

	Fan oven temperature (°C)	Cooking time
Lasagne or cannelloni	190°	½ hour
Garlic bread	190°	¼ hour
Mixed green salad		
Cassata Siciliana		

Prepare the lasagne or cannelloni according to your favourite recipe. Place on the third shelf from the bottom of the oven.

Prepare the garlic bread in the usual way, wrap tightly in kitchen foil and place on the bottom shelf of the oven.

	Fan oven temperature (°C)	Cooking time
Monkfish kebabs	200°	¼ hour
Crispy courgettes (zucchini)	200°	½ hour
Boiled rice		
Baked Alaska	200°	5 minutes

Prepare the monkfish kebabs according to the recipe on page 93.

Prepare the courgettes according to the recipe on page 47. Place the courgettes on the fourth shelf from the bottom of the oven. Place the kebabs on a wire rack over a roasting pan on the second shelf from the bottom of the oven.

Prepare the Baked Alaska according to the recipe on page 96. Place on the third shelf from the bottom of the oven after you have eaten the rest of the meal. Serve immediately after the meringue has browned. (See photograph page 97.)

Monkfish Kebabs (page 93, Crispy Courgettes (page 47)

RECIPES

SNACKS AND
HORS D'OEUVRES

Seafood au Gratin

To serve 4

Ingredients	Metric	Imperial	American
Butter	45 ml	3 tbsp	3 tbsp
Flour	25 g	1 oz	1/4 cup
Curry powder	5 ml	1 tsp	1 tsp
Milk	300 ml	1/2 pt	1 1/4 cups
Tomato purée	30 ml	2 tbsp	2 tbsp
Sherry or brandy	15 ml	1 tbsp	1 tbsp
Salt and black or cayenne pepper			
Prawns (shrimp) or crabmeat	450 g	1 lb	2 cups
Grated cheese	25 g	1 oz	1/4 cup

Melt 25g/1 oz butter and stir in the flour and curry powder until well blended. Cook for 1 minute. Slowly add the milk, stirring constantly, and then the tomato purée. Cook, stirring, until the sauce thickens and comes to the boil. Add the sherry or brandy and season to taste. Stir in the prawns or crabmeat and the remaining butter. Transfer to a greased ovenproof dish or four individual ramekins, sprinkle with cheese and brown. The cheese can be Cheddar, Emmenthal, Gruyère or Parmesan.

To cook conventionally: Brown under the grill (broiler) at its highest temperature setting for 5 minutes or until golden and bubbly.
To cook in a fan oven: Brown at 210° for 5 minutes or until golden and bubbly.

To cook in a multifunction oven: Use the setting for fan + grill and brown at 210° for 5 minutes or until golden.

Variations

Omit the curry powder and stir asparagus tips or chopped hardboiled (hard-cooked) eggs into the sauce along with the prawns or crabmeat. The sauce can also be flavoured with mustard or lightly crushed green peppercorns instead of curry powder.

Enrich the sauce by substituting cream for all or part of the milk. Instead of cooking the Seafood au Gratin in ramekins, spoon carefully into vol au vent cases or baked shells of shortcrust or cheese pastry and heat through gently for 10 minutes at 200° in a conventional oven or 180° in a fan oven. If you are using a multifunction oven, use the setting for fan + bottom and heat the pastry shells for 10 minutes at 180°.

Baked Grapefruit

To serve 2

Ingredients	Metric	Imperial	American
Grapefruit	1	1	1
Curaçao or Cointreau	30 ml	2 tbsp	2 tbsp
Brown or white sugar	10 ml	2 tsp	2 tsp

Cut the grapefruit in half and carefully loosen the sections removing the centre core of pith. Sprinkle with liqueur and sugar. Arrange in ovenproof dishes and serve hot.

To cook conventionally: Pre-heat the oven for 10 minutes. Bake the grapefruit for 10–15 minutes at 190°.
To cook in a fan oven: Pre-heat the oven for 5 minutes. Bake the grapefruit for 10–15 minutes at 170°.
To cook in a multifunction oven: Pre-heat the oven for 5 minutes. Use the setting for fan + grill (broiler) and bake the grapefruit for 10–15 minutes at 170°.

Variations

Substitute honey for sugar and sprinkle some chopped nuts onto each grapefruit half. The liqueur can be omitted and a knob of butter placed on the grapefruit. You can also add a touch of spice with a pinch of ground cinnamon or nutmeg.

Liver Pâté

To serve 4–6

Ingredients	Metric	Imperial	American
Liver	225 g	8 oz	½ lb
Belly pork (fresh bacon)	225 g	8 oz	½ lb
Green peppercorns	15 ml	1 tbsp	1 tbsp
Brandy	15 ml	1 tbsp	1 tbsp
Madeira	50 ml	2 fl oz	¼ cup
Salt	5 ml	1 tsp	1 tsp
Flour	30 ml	2 tbsp	2 tbsp
Dried thyme	2 ½ ml	½ tsp	½ tsp
Egg	1	1	1
Onion	1	1	1
Margarine	15 g	½ oz	1 tbsp
Rashers (slices) bacon	8–10	8–10	8–10
Bay leaf	1	1	1

Mince the liver and belly pork. If you like a very smooth pâté, put the meat through the mincer twice, or mince once and then liquidise. The liver can be pig's, calf's or duck's.

Lightly crush the peppercorns and mix into the liver and pork along with the brandy, Madeira, salt, flour, thyme and lightly beaten egg. Place in a covered dish and refrigerate overnight so that the flavours can develop. Stir occasionally.

Cut the onion in half, slice thinly and brown in the margarine.

Stretch the bacon rashers with the flat side of a sharp knife and line a loaf pan or round porcelain dish. To check the seasoning in the pâté, lightly fry a small spoonful in vegetable oil until it is firm. Taste and adjust the seasoning in the pâté mixture if necessary. Spread half of the pâté mixture over the bacon, sprinkle with onions and top with the remaining pâté. Place the bay leaf in the centre. Cover with a double layer of kitchen foil. Place the dish in a roasting pan half filled with hot water.

The pâté will be ready when the juices are clear and a skewer inserted in the centre comes out clean. Cooking time may vary slightly according to the depth of the pan you use.

Cool the pâté completely, wrap in foil and leave overnight before serving.

If you want to keep the pâté for a few days, pour a thin layer of clarified butter over the surface after the pâté has cooled. Refrigerate for up to one week.

To cook conventionally: Bake the pâté for 1 ¼ hours at 160°.
To cook in a fan oven: Bake the pâté for 1 hour at 140°.
To cook in a multifunction oven: Use the setting for fan or conventional cooking only and proceed as above.

Variations
Place a layer of hazelnuts, sliced pork or sautéed mushrooms in the middle of the pâté mixture. If you are using duck liver, arrange a layer of cooked duck meat in the middle.

Juniper berries can be used instead of green peppercorns.

Spiced Nuts

To serve 4–8

Ingredients	Metric	Imperial	American
Egg whites OR	2	2	2
Butter	50 g	2 oz	¼ cup
Caster (superfine) sugar	175 g	6 oz	¾ cup
Salt	2 ½ ml	½ tsp	½ tsp
Curry powder	5 ml	1 tsp	1 tsp
Ground cloves	2 ½ ml	½ tsp	½ tsp
Cinnamon	5 ml	1 tsp	1 tsp
Ground nutmeg	1 ¼ ml	¼ tsp	¼ tsp
Ground allspice	1 ¼ ml	¼ tsp	¼ tsp
Shelled nuts	450 g	1 lb	1 lb

Lightly beat the egg whites or melt the butter. Combine the sugar, salt and spices. Dip the nuts first in the egg white or butter and then in the spices. You can use one or more kinds of nuts, made up from walnuts, almonds, peanuts, pecans or brazil nuts. Shake off the excess spice mixture and spread the nuts on a baking tray.

When the nuts have cooled they can be stored in an airtight tin.

To cook conventionally: Bake the nuts at 140° for 45 minutes.
To cook in a fan oven: Bake the nuts at 130° for 45 minutes.
To cook in a multifunction oven: Use the setting for fan + bottom and bake the nuts at 130° for 45 minutes.

Variations
Omit the curry powder or substitute chilli powder, cayenne pepper, Tabasco (hot pepper sauce) or Worcestershire sauce.

Sprinkle the nuts with a mixture of salt, celery salt and garlic powder with or without a pinch of ground cumin and/or chilli powder. Bake as above.

Savoury Crackers

Ingredients	Metric	Imperial	American
Plain (all-purpose) flour	75 g	3 oz	¾ cup
Salt	2 ½ ml	½ tsp	½ tsp
Mustard powder (optional)	2 ½ ml	½ tsp	½ tsp
Sesame seeds	30 ml	2 tbsp	2 tbsp
Butter OR	75 g	3 oz	6 tbsp
Sesame oil AND	15 ml	1 tbsp	1 tbsp
Egg	1	1	1
Cheese (optional)	75 g	3 oz	¾ cup

Combine the flour, salt and mustard powder if you are using it. The flour can be white, wholewheat or a mixture. Stir in half of the sesame seeds. Rub in the butter or sesame oil until the mixture resembles coarse breadcrumbs. If you are using oil you will need the lightly beaten egg to bind the mixture, otherwise you can gently press it together with your fingertips to form a dough. Knead in the grated cheese using any variety you have to hand. Cheddar, Leicester, Edam, Gruyère or Emmenthal are all suitable.

Wrap the dough in clingfilm and chill for 1 hour.

Roll the dough until it is approximately ¾ cm/¼ inch thick and cut into squares, circles or triangles. Place on a greased baking tray and sprinkle with the remaining sesame seeds.

To cook conventionally: Bake the biscuits at 190° for 10–15 minutes or until crisp and golden.

To cook in a fan oven: Bake the biscuits at 170° for 10–15 minutes or until crisp and golden.

To cook in a multifunction oven: Use the setting for fan or conventional cooking only and proceed as above. Fan cooking will produce a more tender cracker, conventional cooking will produce a brown and crisp cracker.

Toasted Cheese Snacks

To serve 4

Ingredients	Metric	Imperial	American
Slices bread	4–8	4–8	4–8
Butter for spreading			
Slices salami	4	4	4
or ham			
Cheese	125 g	4 oz	1 cup
Tomatoes	2	2	2
Dried oregano			
or basil	10 ml	2 tsp	2 tsp

To make open sandwiches, toast the bread on one side only.
Spread with butter (plain or flavoured) and arrange a slice of
salami or ham on each. Cover with grated cheese, top with
two tomato slices per slice of bread and sprinkle with oregano
or basil. Place the bread on a wire rack over a roasting pan.
Toast until the cheese has melted.

   To make closed sandwiches, spread one side of each slice
of bread with butter. Place four slices, buttered side down, on

a wire rack over a roasting pan. Assemble the sandwiches as above, finishing with a second slice of bread, buttered side up. Toast until the cheese has melted and the bread is golden.

To cook conventionally: Use the highest grill (broiler) setting. If you are making closed sandwiches, turn them over when the top slice of bread is crisp and brown.

To cook in a fan oven: Toast the sandwiches for 5 minutes at 220°. There is no need to turn closed sandwiches.

To cook in a multifunction oven: Use the setting for fan + grill. Toast the sandwiches for 5 minutes at 220°. If you are making closed sandwiches, turn them over when the top slice of bread is crisp and brown.

Hot Garlic Spread

To serve 4

Ingredients	Metric	Imperial	American
Bulbs garlic	2	2	2
Butter	15 g	½ oz	1 tbsp
Chicken stock	15 ml	1 tbsp	1 tbsp
Fresh rosemary	5 ml	1 tsp	1 tsp
Salt and pepper			

Remove only the loose outer skin of the garlic heads, but do not separate or peel the cloves. Place in a shallow ovenproof dish or individual ramekins. Sprinkle with melted butter, stock, rosemary, salt and pepper. If you use dried rosemary, use 2 ½ ml/½ tsp only.

To serve, separate the cloves and pinch to remove the skin. Spread the cooked garlic on French bread, biscuits or raw vegetables.

To cook conventionally: Bake the garlic for 1 ¼ hours at 140°. Baste frequently.

To cook in a fan oven: Bake the garlic for 1 hour at 130°. Baste frequently.

To cook in a multifunction oven: Use the setting for fan or conventional cooking only and proceed as above.

Stuffed Bacon Savouries

To serve 4

Ingredients	Metric	Imperial	American
Rashers (slices) streaky bacon	4	4	4
Prunes, oysters, snails, chicken livers, pineapple cubes or chunks of cheese	8	8	8

Cut each rasher of bacon in half. Gently stretch with the flat side of a knife so that each rasher is as thin as possible.

Wrap the prunes, oysters, snails, livers, fruit or cheese in bacon. Fasten with a toothpick or bamboo skewer, place on a wire rack over a grill (broiler) pan and cook until the bacon is crisp. Serve immediately on buttered toast or crusty French bread.

To cook conventionally: Grill (broil) on the highest setting possible, turning occasionally.
To cook in a fan oven: Grill for 5–10 minutes at 220°. There is no need to turn.
To cook in a multifunction oven: Use the setting for fan + grill and cook the bacon for 5–10 minutes at 220°, turning occasionally.

Variations
Soak the prunes in port overnight before using. Snails can be marinated in white wine and garlic overnight.

VEGETABLE AND VEGETARIAN DISHES

Pumpkin Gratin

To serve 4

Ingredients	Metric	Imperial	American
Salt pork	125 g	4 oz	¼ lb
Pumpkin	1 ½ kg	3 lb	3 lb
Cloves garlic	3	3	3
Fresh parsley	15 ml	1 tbsp	1 tbsp
Olive oil	30 ml	2 tbsp	2 tbsp

Cut the pork into very small pieces and sauté until crisp and golden. Drain well. If you prefer, smoked bacon can be substituted, or diced, cooked ham. The ham does not need to be sautéed.

Weigh the pumpkin after the skin and seeds have been removed. Cut into small cubes. Toss with the crushed garlic and chopped parsley. Mix in the pork or bacon.

Brush the surface of an ovenproof casserole with olive oil. Place the pumpkin mixture in the casserole and sprinkle the surface with olive oil.

To cook conventionally: Bake the pumpkin gratin at 160° for 1 ¾ hours or until the pumpkin is soft and the crust brown.

To cook in a fan oven: Bake the pumpkin gratin at 150° for 1 ½ hours or until the pumpkin is soft and the crust brown.

To cook in a multifunction oven: Use the setting for fan or conventional cooking only and cook as above but switch to the setting for fan + grill (broiler) for the last 15 minutes.

Broad Beans with Rice

To serve 4–6

Ingredients	Metric	Imperial	American
Rashers (slices) streaky bacon	4	4	4
Butter	50 g	2 oz	¼ cup
Medium onion OR	1	1	1
Spring onions (scallions)	4	4	4
Cloves garlic	2	2	2
Broad (lima) beans	225 g	8 oz	½ lb
Pine kernels or flaked almonds	50 g	2 oz	½ cup
Long grain rice	225 g	8 oz	1 cup + 2 tbsp
Boiling water or chicken stock	575 ml	1 pint	2 ½ cups
Fresh rosemary	1¼ ml	¼ tsp	¼ tsp

Fry the diced bacon in melted butter until it is crisp. Drain well and transfer to a large ovenproof casserole.

Soften the chopped onion or spring onions and garlic in the remaining fat. Drain and add to the bacon. Toss the broad beans and pine kernels or almonds in the fat for 1–2 minutes so that they are well coated. Add the rice and stir to coat. Mix with the bacon in the casserole. Top with water or stock, cover and cook until the liquid has been absorbed. Check halfway through the cooking time and add a little bit more water if necessary.

Sprinkle with chopped rosemary just before serving.

To cook conventionally: Bake the rice for 40 minutes at 160°.
To cook in a fan oven: Bake the rice for 40 minutes at 140°.
To cook in a multifunction oven: Use the setting for fan or conventional cooking only and proceed as above.

Variations

Use brown rice, white rice or a mixture. You can also add a little bit of wild rice to make an additional contrast in flavour and texture.

Cook the rice as instructed, cool and use to stuff tomatoes or green peppers. Sprinkle with olive oil or 30 ml/2 tbsp well flavoured tomato sauce and bake in a shallow dish for 1 hour at 190° in a conventional oven or 170° in a fan or multifunction oven.

Hot Pepper Soufflé

To serve 4

Ingredients	Metric	Imperial	American
Butter	25 g	1 oz	2 tbsp
Flour	15 ml	1 tbsp	1 tbsp
Milk	300 ml	½ pt	1 ¼ cups
Strong cheese	125 g	4 oz	1 cup
Eggs, separated	3	3	3
Hot pepper sauce	few drops	few drops	few drops
Parmesan cheese	15 ml	1 tbsp	1 tbsp

Melt the butter and stir in the flour until it is completely absorbed. Cook for 2–3 minutes. Slowly add the milk, stirring constantly, until the sauce thickens and comes to the boil. Simmer gently for 2–3 minutes.

Grate the strongest cheese you can find — mature Cheddar is particularly good. Add to the sauce and continue to cook until the cheese has melted. Remove from the heat.

Add the egg yolks, one at a time, to the sauce. Mix well after adding each one. Season to taste with either Tabasco, chilli and garlic or West Indian hot pepper sauce. If you can get Mexican jalapeno peppers, use these instead. Remove the seeds and chop finely. If none of these ingredients is available, substitute a pinch of cayenne pepper.

Whisk the egg whites until they are stiff but not dry. Carefully fold into the cheese sauce, starting with just one spoonful and gradually adding the remainder. Pour into a greased 1 litre/2 pint/2½ pint soufflé dish, sprinkle with Parmesan cheese and bake until well risen and golden. Serve the soufflé immediately.

To cook conventionally: Bake for 45 minutes at 180°.
To cook in a fan oven: Bake for 35 minutes at 170°.
To cook in a multifunction oven: Use the setting for fan + bottom. Bake the soufflé for 35 minutes at 170°.

Crispy Courgettes

To serve 4

Ingredients	Metric	Imperial	American
Courgettes (zucchini)	4	4	4
Olive oil	50 ml	2 fl oz	¼ cup
Salt and pepper			
Breadcrumbs	50 g	2 oz	1 cup
Cloves garlic	2	2	2
Fresh basil	10 ml	2 tsp	2 tsp
Fresh parsley	10 ml	2 tsp	2 tsp
Pine kernels	50 g	2 oz	½ cup

Wash and trim the courgettes. Cut in half lengthways and brown in hot oil. Drain well and arrange in a single layer in a shallow ovenproof dish. Season with salt and pepper.

Toss the breadcrumbs, crushed garlic, chopped herbs and pine kernels in the remaining oil until they are moist. If you cannot get fresh herbs, use dried but cut the quantity in half.

Sprinkle the crumbs over the courgettes and drizzle with olive oil.

To cook conventionally: Bake for 20 minutes at 250°.
To cook in a fan oven: Bake for 20 minutes at 225°.
To cook in a multifunction oven: Use the setting for fan + grill (broiler). Bake the courgettes for 20 minutes at 225°.

Variations

Prepare the courgettes as above. Soften a finely chopped onion with the garlic in the oil, add 450 g/1 lb chopped tomatoes or tomato sauce (Passata) and season with herbs. Pour over the courgettes, sprinkle with breadcrumbs and bake as above.

Sliced tomatoes or mushrooms can be treated in a similar way by alternating layers of tomato or mushrooms and crumbs, finishing with a layer of crumbs. You can also use the crumbs to stuff hollowed out tomatoes or mushrooms for baking.

(*Illustrated on p. 33*)

Scrambled Egg Supper

To serve 4

Ingredients	Metric	Imperial	American
Broccoli	225 g	8 oz	½ lb
Slices bread	8	8	8
Butter for spreading and Butter	75 g	3 oz	6 tbsp
Flour	15 ml	1 tbsp	1 tbsp
Milk	300 ml	½ pt	1 ¼ cups
Cheese	50 g	2 oz	½ cup
Salt and pepper			
Eggs	8	8	8
Double (heavy) cream	30 ml	2 tbsp	2 tbsp

Cook the broccoli until it is soft, drain well and set aside.

Spread both sides of the bread with butter. Sprinkle with crushed garlic if you like. You can use either French bread, crusty rolls or slices from a sandwich loaf. Grill (broil) as directed.

Melt 25 g/1 oz/2 tbsp butter and stir in the flour. Slowly add the milk and cook, stirring constantly, until the sauce thickens. Stir in the grated cheese (Cheddar, Leicester, or Double Gloucester) and season to taste with salt and pepper.

Whisk the eggs with the cream. Season with salt and pepper. Scramble the eggs in the remaining butter.

Arrange the broccoli on the cooked croutons, top with scrambled eggs and finish off with a spoonful of cheese sauce. Grill until bubbling and golden. Serve with a grilled tomato.

To cook conventionally: Grill the croutons on the maximum setting, turning once. Grill the assembled dish for 5 minutes on maximum.

To cook in a fan oven: Grill the croutons on a wire rack over a baking tray at 200° until crisp and brown. Do not turn. Grill the assembled dish for 5 minutes at 200°.

To cook in a multifunction oven: Use the setting for fan only to grill the croutons as above. Use the setting for fan + grill for the assembled dish.

Variations

Place a slice of ham on each crouton before the broccoli, or mix diced ham into the eggs before scrambling them.

Substitute Quick Hollandaise sauce for the cheese sauce. Heat 30 ml/2 tbsp lemon juice with 15 ml/1 tbsp white wine vinegar and slowly add to a liquidiser or food processor in which you have already whisked 3 egg yolks with a pinch of salt and 5 ml/1 tsp sugar. Slowly add 175 g/6 oz/¾ cup melted butter and process until smooth and light.

Substitute Cream Cheese Sauce for the sauce above. Heat 75 ml/3 fl oz/⅓ cup milk with 125 g/4 oz/½ cup cream cheese and season with salt, pepper, crushed garlic and a spoonful of Parmesan cheese.

Spinach Pie

To serve 4–6

Ingredients	Metric	Imperial	American
Puff pastry	350 g	12 oz	¾ lb
New potatoes	350 g	12 oz	¾ lb
Salt and pepper			
Fresh spinach	450 g	1 lb	1 lb
Mozzarella cheese	225 g	8 oz	½ lb
Egg	1	1	1

Cut the pastry into two pieces, one twice as large as the other. Roll out to make large circles and leave to rest for 10 minutes. Use the larger piece to line the base and sides of a 20 cm/8 inch loose-bottomed sandwich tin (pan).

Boil the potatoes until they are just tender. Cool, peel and slice thickly. Arrange a layer of potatoes in the bottom of the pastry-lined tin and season with salt and pepper.

Cook the spinach. You can boil or steam it or cook it gently in a covered pan with a knob of butter. Drain very well, season and arrange a layer over the potatoes. Top with sliced cheese and a final layer of potatoes.

Use the remaining piece of pastry to make a lid for the pie, sealing it well with lightly beaten egg. Decorate the top with shapes cut from the pastry trimmings, cut a hole so that the steam can escape and glaze with egg.

To cook conventionally: Bake the pie at 220° for 25 minutes or until the pastry is crisp and brown.
To cook in a fan oven: Bake the pie at 200° for 25 minutes or until the pastry is crisp and brown.
To cook in a multifunction oven: Use the setting for fan or conventional cooking only and proceed as above. The pastry will be golden and tender if cooked on the fan only setting or dark and crispy if baked on the setting for conventional cooking.

Variations
Substitute Swiss chard for all or part of the spinach.

Gruyère cheese can be substituted for Mozzarella.

Baked Cauliflower Layer

To serve 4

Ingredients	Metric	Imperial	American
Medium cauliflower	1	1	1
Potatoes	450 g	1 lb	1 lb
Salt and pepper			
Hardboiled (hard-cooked) eggs	4	4	4
Butter	75 g	3 oz	6 tbsp
Cornflour (cornstarch)	15 ml	3 tsp	3 tsp
Mustard	5 ml	1 tsp	1 tsp
Natural yoghurt or sour cream	300 ml	½ pint	1 ¼ cups
Edam or Gruyère, grated	125 g	4 oz	1 cup

Separate the cauliflower into small pieces and cook until tender. Drain well. Scrub the potatoes and cook until tender. Cool, peel and slice.

Arrange a layer of potatoes in a well greased ovenproof dish. Season with salt and pepper. Top with a layer of sliced eggs and cauliflower. Season to taste. Finish with the remaining potatoes.

Melt the butter and stir in the cornflour, mustard and yoghurt or sour cream. Heat until the sauce thickens slightly. Pour over the vegetables and sprinkle with grated cheese.

To cook conventionally: Bake the Cauliflower Layer for 15 minutes at 200°.
To cook in a fan oven: Bake the Cauliflower Layer for 15 minutes at 180°.
To cook in a multifunction oven: Use the setting for fan + grill (broiler). Bake the Cauliflower Layer for 15 minutes at 180°.

Variations
Add a layer of sautéed leeks, fennel, mushrooms or courgettes (zucchini).

Substitute Blue Stilton, Cheddar or Red Leicester for Edam or Gruyère.

Potato Roulade

To serve 4

Ingredients	Metric	Imperial	American
Leeks	175 g	6 oz	6 oz
Potatoes	225 g	8 oz	½ lb
Plain (all-purpose) flour	125 g	4 oz	1 cup
Salt	pinch	pinch	pinch
Baking powder	10 ml	2 tsp	2 tsp
Margarine	50 g	2 oz	¼ cup
Cheese, grated	50 g	2 oz	½ cup
Milk	120 ml	4 fl oz	½ cup
Eggs, separated	2	2	2

Clean the leeks, cut into 1¼ cm/½ inch slices and boil until soft. Drain well.

Peel, dice and boil the potatoes. Mash until smooth and mix with the leeks.

Combine the flour, salt and baking powder. Rub in the margarine until the mixture resembles coarse breadcrumbs. Stir in the grated cheese. You can use mature Cheddar, Red Leicester, Wensleydale or whatever else is available. Stir in the potatoes, milk and egg yolks.

Whisk the egg whites until they are stiff but not dry. Gently fold into the potato mixture, starting with just one spoonful and gradually adding the remainder. Carefully turn onto a greased Swiss roll tin (jelly roll pan) that has been lined with buttered vegetable parchment or greaseproof (waxed) paper.

When the roulade is firm to the touch, turn out onto a clean sheet of parchment or greaseproof paper. Spread with a white sauce, flavoured to taste (i.e. curry powder, cheese, herbs, wine etc.) and top with a mixture of sautéed vegetables, seafood or cooked poultry. Roll, coat with a little more sauce and place on a large serving dish. Brown quickly. Serve garnished with asparagus spears, courgettes (zucchini) or grilled (broiled) tomatoes and mushrooms.

To cook conventionally: Bake the roulade at 200° for 15

minutes. Brown the assembled roulade for 2–3 minutes at 220°.

To cook in a fan oven: Bake the roulade at 190° for 15 minutes. Brown the assembled roulade for 2–3 minutes at 210°.

To cook in a multifunction oven: Use the setting for fan or conventional cooking only and proceed as above. Use the setting for fan + grill to brown the assembled roulade.

Variations

Substitute chopped spinach or grated courgettes (zucchini) for the leeks. Use Edam, Emmenthal, Parmesan or Gruyère instead of English cheese. Flavour the roulade with dried mustard or herbs to taste.

Braised Red Cabbage

To serve 4–6

Ingredients	Metric	Imperial	American
Chicken, bacon or pork fat	50 g	2 oz	4 tbsp
Sugar	30 ml	2 tbsp	2 tbsp
Onion	1	1	1
Red cabbage	450 g	1 lb	1 lb
Cooking apples	2	2	2
Wine vinegar	30 ml	2 tbsp	2 tbsp
Caraway seeds	5 ml	1 tsp	1 tsp

Heat the fat and stir in the sugar until it begins to brown.
Add the finely chopped onion and cook, stirring constantly,
until golden. Mix in the shredded or grated cabbage and
diced apples. Sprinkle with vinegar and caraway seeds.
Transfer to a casserole and cover.

To cook conventionally: Braise the cabbage at 160° for 45
minutes or until soft. If it begins to dry out, add a little water.
To cook in a fan oven: Braise the cabbage at 140° for 35
minutes or until soft. If it begins to dry out, add a little water.
To cook in a multifunction oven: Use the setting for fan or
conventional cooking only and proceed as above.

Variation
To braise white cabbage, brown the onion in vegetable oil
rather than fat, stir in the cabbage and season with either
cumin seeds or a mixture of crushed juniper berries and
garlic. Omit all the other ingredients.

Peperonata Hero

To serve 4

Ingredients	Metric	Imperial	American
Olive oil	75 ml	3 fl oz	1/3 cup
Onions	450 g	1 lb	1 lb
Cloves garlic	2	2	2
Peppers	2	2	2
Courgettes (zucchini)	2	2	2
Aubergine (eggplant)	1	1	1
Salt and pepper			
Dried oregano	5 ml	1 tsp	1 tsp
Dried basil	5 ml	1 tsp	1 tsp
French loaf	1	1	1

Heat the olive oil in the bottom of an ovenproof casserole.
Add the sliced onions and crushed garlic. Cut the peppers
into thin strips. You can use red or green peppers, or one of
each. Cut the courgettes and aubergine into quarters
lengthways and then into thin strips. Place all of the
vegetables in the casserole and mix well. Add the salt, pepper
and herbs. Cover and cook as below.

Cut the top off the French loaf and scoop out the soft
centre. Fill with cooked vegetables, replace the top of the
bread and wrap in kitchen foil. Place the loaf on a baking tray
and return to the oven until hot and crispy.

To cook conventionally: Braise the vegetables for 1 hour at
180°. Bake the filled Hero for 15 minutes at 190°.
To cook in a fan oven: Braise the vegetables for 1 hour at
170°. Bake the filled Hero for 15 minutes at 170°.
To cook in a multifunction oven: Use the setting for fan or
conventional cooking only and proceed as above.

Candied Carrots

To serve 4

Ingredients	Metric	Imperial	American
Carrots	675 g	1 ½ lb	1 ½ lb
Brown sugar	15 ml	1 tbsp	1 tbsp
Honey or golden (corn) syrup	15 ml	1 tbsp	1 tbsp
Chicken stock	120 ml	4 fl oz	½ cup

Peel and slice or dice the carrots. Blanch in boiling water for 5 minutes. Drain and transfer to an ovenproof dish. Mix in the sugar, honey or syrup and stock. Cover and check occasionally to ensure that the liquid doesn't get completely absorbed — the carrots should be just moist.

To cook conventionally: Bake the carrots for 2 hours at 150°.
To cook in a fan oven: Bake the carrots for 1½ hours at 130°
To cook in a multifunction oven: Use the setting for fan or conventional cooking only and proceed as above.

Variation
Omit the sugar and honey or syrup. Flavour the carrots with grated lemon rind and/or caraway seeds.

Potato Soufflé

To serve 4

Ingredients	Metric	Imperial	American
Potatoes	900 g	2 lb	2 lb
Sour cream, yoghurt or quark	30 ml	2 tbsp	2 tbsp
Single (light) cream	30 ml	2 tbsp	2 tbsp
Eggs, separated	2	2	2
Fresh parsley	30 ml	2 tbsp	2 tbsp
Salt and pepper			
Curd cheese	125 g	4 oz	½ cup

Peel, dice and boil the potatoes until they are tender. Drain well and mash with the sour cream, yoghurt or quark and single cream. Add the lightly beaten egg yolks, chopped parsley and salt and pepper. Mix well. Fold in the curd cheese.

Whisk the egg whites until they are stiff but not dry. Gently add to the potatoes, starting with just one spoonful and gradually adding the remainder. Pour into a greased soufflé dish.

To cook conventionally: Bake the soufflé for 30 minutes at 180°.
To cook in a fan oven: Bake the soufflé for 30 minutes at 170°.
To cook in a multifunction oven: Use the setting for fan or conventional cooking only and proceed as above. The setting for conventional cooking will produce a browner crust.

MEAT

Lamb with Chickpeas and Apricots

To serve 4

Ingredients	Metric	Imperial	American
Chickpeas	225 g	8 oz	1/2 lb
Onion	1	1	1
Oil	30 ml	2 tbsp	2 tbsp
Boned lamb	900 g	2 lb	2 lb
Dried apricots	50 g	2 oz	1/3 cup
Cinnamon	2 1/2 ml	1/2 tsp	1/2 tsp
Ground coriander	2 1/2 ml	1/2 tsp	1/2 tsp
Split peas	50 g	2 oz	1/4 cup
Water	575 ml	1 pint	2 1/2 cups

Soak the chickpeas for 1 hour in enough boiling water to cover them, or soak overnight in cold water. Drain well, cover with fresh water and cook until tender. This will take approximately 1 hour, or 15 minutes if you use a pressure cooker. Drain and leave to cool. If you prefer, tinned chickpeas can be substituted — simply drain, rinse and drain.

Soften the finely chopped onion in hot oil. Add the diced lamb and stir until sealed on all sides. Drain well and transfer to an ovenproof casserole. The lamb can be from either a leg or shoulder, but stewing lamb or neck cutlets can also be used. In this case, allow extra weight to compensate for the bones.

Dice the apricots and add to the lamb along with the spices, split peas and water. Mix well.

To cook conventionally: Bake for 2 hours at 180°. Add the chickpeas, mix well and cook for an additional 30 minutes.
To cook in a fan oven: Bake for 1 1/2 hours at 160°. Add the chickpeas, mix well and cook for an additional 30 minutes.
To cook in a multifunction oven: Use the setting for fan or conventional cooking only and proceed as above.

(Illustrated on p. 4)

Braised Lamb in Tomato Sauce

To serve 4

Ingredients	Metric	Imperial	American
Lamb chops or cutlets	4	4	4
Clove garlic	1	1	1
Oil	30 ml	2 tbsp	2 tbsp
Sauce			
Tomato purée	60 ml	4 tbsp	4 tbsp
Stock, cider or red wine	150 ml	5 fl oz	⅔ cup
Small onion	1	1	1
Nutmeg	pinch	pinch	pinch
Rosemary or thyme	1 sprig	1 sprig	1 sprig
Sugar	2 ½ ml	½ tsp	½ tsp
Salt and pepper			

Rub each chop or cutlet with the cut side of the garlic and leave for an hour or longer. Brush with oil and brown on both sides. Arrange in a single layer in a shallow dish.

Combine all the ingredients for the sauce and simmer gently for 15 minutes. Strain the sauce and season to taste with salt and pepper. Pour over the lamb. Cook as below and serve with macaroni tossed with butter, Parmesan cheese and fresh parsley.

To cook conventionally: Bake for 1 ¼ hours at 160°.
To cook in a fan oven: Bake for 1 hour at 140°.
To cook in a multifunction oven: Use the setting for fan or conventional cooking only and proceed as above.

Variation
Prepare Osso Bucco with the same sauce. Dust veal shanks or shin of veal in seasoned flour, brown on all sides and braise in the sauce as above. Sprinkle with finely chopped parsley, garlic and lemon rind just before serving.

Lamb Biryani

To serve 6

Ingredients	Metric	Imperial	American
Onions	4	4	4
Oil	50 ml	2 fl oz	¼ cup
Boned lamb	900 g	2 lb	2 lb
Chillis	1–2	1–2	1–2
Cloves garlic	3	3	3
Cardamom pods	6	6	6
Cinnamon	2 ½ ml	½ tsp	½ tsp
Ground coriander	2 ½ ml	½ tsp	½ tsp
Ground cumin	2 ½ ml	½ tsp	½ tsp
Ground cloves	2 ½ ml	½ tsp	½ tsp
Ground ginger	1 ¼ ml	¼ tsp	¼ tsp
Lemon juice	15 ml	1 tbsp	1 tbsp
Natural yoghurt	300 ml	½ pt	1 ¼ cups
Salt	5 ml	1 tsp	1 tsp
Saffron threads	5 ml	1 tsp	1 tsp
Hot milk or water	30 ml	2 tbsp	2 tbsp
Rice	450 g	1 lb	1 lb
Water	2 litres	4 pints	5 pts

Slice two of the onions and brown in hot oil. Drain well and transfer to an ovenproof casserole.

Toss the diced lamb in the hot oil until it is sealed on all sides. Drain and add to the onions.

Remove the seeds from the chillis and liquidise along with the remaining two onions, garlic, spices, lemon juice and yoghurt to make a thick paste. Stir into the lamb and onion mixture. Cover the dish and cook as directed below. When the meat is tender, drain well but reserve the cooking liquid. Add salt to taste.

While the meat is cooking, soak the saffron threads in milk or water. Cook the rice in boiling salted water for 5 minutes. Drain well.

To assemble the Biryani, sprinkle 30 ml/2 tbsp oil in the bottom of a large casserole. Arrange alternate layers of rice and meat in the dish, ending with a layer of rice. Carefully pour over the dissolved saffron and the liquid from the meat. Cover the dish and cook as below.

Serve the Biryani garnished with fried onions, chopped green pepper, hardboiled (hard-cooked) eggs and 30 ml/2 tbsp each raisins and almonds lightly browned in vegetable oil.

To cook conventionally: Bake the meat for 40 minutes at 170°. After assembling the Biryani, bake for 30 minutes at 190°.
To cook with a fan oven: Bake the meat for 40 minutes at 160°. After assembling the Biryani, bake for 30 minutes at 180°.
To cook with a multifunction oven: Use the programme for fan or conventional cooking only and proceed as above.

Beef with Aubergine and Okra

To serve 4–6

Ingredients	Metric	Imperial	American
Large aubergine (eggplant)	1	1	1
Chickpeas OR	125 g	4 oz	1/4 lb
Tin chickpeas	439 g	15 1/2 oz	1 lb
Medium onions	2	2	2
Oil	30 ml	2 tbsp	2 tbsp
Stewing steak	900 g	2 lb	2 lb
Tomatoes	4	4	4
Okra	225 g	8 oz	1/2 lb
Tomato purée	15 ml	1 tbsp	1 tbsp
Lemon juice	30 ml	2 tbsp	2 tbsp
Ground cumin	2 1/2 ml	1/2 tsp	1/2 tsp
Salt and pepper			
Water	350 ml	12 fl oz	1 1/2 cups

Cut the aubergine in half lengthways and then in half again. Cut into slices 1 cm/½ inch thick. Sprinkle with salt and leave to drain for 30 minutes.

If you are using uncooked chickpeas, cover them with boiling water and leave to soak for 1 hour. Drain well, cover with fresh water and cook for 1 hour, or 15 minutes if you are using a pressure cooker. Drain and leave to cool. For tinned chickpeas, drain, rinse with cold water and drain again.

Soften the finely chopped onion in hot oil. Add the cubed meat and stir until well sealed. Drain and transfer to an overproof dish.

Plunge the tomatoes into boiling water for 1 minute, then remove and skin. Chop roughly and add to the casserole with the meat.

Carefully wash the okra and remove the tips and stems. If they are large, cut them in half. Add to the casserole.

Pat the aubergine pieces dry with kitchen towel and add to the casserole. Stir in the tomato purée, lemon juice, cumin, salt and pepper. Add the water and mix well. Cover tightly.

To cook conventionally: Bake for 3 hours at 170°. Add the chickpeas 10 minutes before the casserole is ready to serve so that they can be thoroughly heated.

To cook in a fan oven: Bake for 2 ½ hours at 150°. Add the chickpeas as above.

To cook in a multifunction oven: Use the setting for fan or conventional cooking only and proceed as above.

Skewered Meatballs

To serve 4

Ingredients	Metric	Imperial	American
Minced (ground) lamb, beef or pork	450 g	1 lb	1 lb
Flour	30 ml	2 tbsp	2 tbsp
Onion	1	1	1
Clove garlic	1	1	1
Fresh coriander or parsley	30 ml	2 tbsp	2 tbsp
Fresh ginger	5 ml	1 tsp	1 tsp
Salt	5 ml	1 tsp	1 tsp
Garam masala	5 ml	1 tsp	1 tsp
Natural yoghurt	50 ml	2 fl oz	¼ cup

Combine the minced meat with the flour, finely chopped onion, garlic and coriander or parsley. Grate the ginger and add to the meat along with the salt and garam masala. If you cannot find garam masala, substitute mild curry powder. Mix

very well. Shape into eight sausages and gently pass skewers through them. You must use flat or rectangular
skewers so that the meatballs do not revolve when you are turning them. If you cannot get the right skewers, shape the meat into patties as for hamburgers.

Lightly whisk the yoghurt and brush over the meatballs. Arrange on a rack over a roasting tin.

To cook conventionally: Grill (broil) on the highest temperature setting, turning occasionally, and basting with yoghurt each time, for approximately 15 minutes or until the meatballs are brown and thoroughly cooked.

To cook in a fan oven: Grill at 210° for 15 minutes or until the meatballs are brown and thoroughly cooked. There is no need to turn.

To cook in a multifunction oven: Use the setting for fan + grill. Grill the meatballs at 210° for 15 minutes or until they are brown and thoroughly cooked, turning and basting occasionally.

Variations

Vary the flavourings for the meat as you like — to make Italian meatballs, use basil and oregano; to make Chinese meatballs, use a few drops of soy sauce; for Middle Eastern meatballs, use cinnamon and/or mint; to make Swedish meatballs, substitute minced (ground) veal for part of the other meat and flavour with nutmeg or mace.

To stretch the meat, add 50 g/ 2 oz/ 1 cup breadcrumbs or bread soaked in milk and bind with a lightly beaten egg.

Instead of grilling the meatballs, they can be browned first in a very little oil and then cooked gently in any kind of sauce you like, for example tomato, cream or sweet and sour. Put the meatballs into a covered casserole, add the sauce and bake for 45 - 60 minutes according to their size (small meatballs can be served with cocktails or as part of a buffet) at 200° in a conventional oven or 180° in a fan oven. If you have a multifunction oven, use the setting for fan or conventional cooking only.

Cassoulet

To serve 8

Ingredients	Metric	Imperial	American
Dried haricot (navy) beans	900 g	2 lb	2 lb
Cloves garlic	2	2	2
Onions	3	3	3
Bouquet garni	1	1	1
Salt pork, fat bacon or streaky rashers (slices)	450 g	1 lb	1 lb
Duck quarters	2	2	2
Boned lamb	450 g	1 lb	1 lb
Stick celery	1	1	1
Tomatoes	450 g	1 lb	1 lb
Dry white wine	50 ml	2 fl oz	¼ cup
Salt and pepper			
Smoked garlic sausage	450 g	1 lb	1 lb
White breadcrumbs	50 g	2 oz	1 cup

Soak the haricot beans for 1 hour in enough boiling water to cover them, or soak overnight in cold water. Drain well, cover with fresh water or chicken stock and bring to the boil. Skim, add the garlic cloves, one of the onions, the bouquet garni and the pork, fat bacon or rolled up bacon rashers. Simmer until the beans are tender but do not let them split. This will take approximately 1 hour, or 15 minutes if you are using a pressure cooker. Drain the beans, reserve liquid.

Roast or grill (broil) the duck quarters. Cool, reserve fat.

Brown the diced lamb in 30 ml/2 tbsp duck fat. Drain and transfer to a suitable dish for the oven. Chop the remaining onions and brown with the chopped celery in the fat left in the pan. Drain and add to the lamb.

Plunge the tomatoes into boiling water for 1 minute. Remove from the water, skin and chop roughly. Add to the lamb with the wine and salt and pepper. Cover and bake.

Brush the bottom of a large casserole with 15 ml/1 tbsp duck fat. Arrange a layer of beans in the bottom of the dish. Top with slices of garlic sausage, chunks of duck, lamb and pork or bacon. Add another layer of beans. Continue until all the ingredients have been used, ending with a layer of beans. Moisten with the reserved liquid. Sprinkle a layer of breadcrumbs over the beans and drizzle with duck fat. The crust can be stirred into the Cassoulet once or twice while baking and more crumbs added. Add extra liquid if the Cassoulet gets too dry.

To cook conventionally: Grill the duck portions on a wire rack over a roasting pan for 15 minutes on the highest temperature setting. Turn frequently. Bake the lamb mixture for 1 hour at 180°. Bake the Cassoulet for 2 hours at 190°.

To cook in a fan oven: Roast the duck portions on a wire rack over a roasting pan for 15 minutes at 180°. Do not turn. Bake the lamb mixture for 50 minutes at 160°. Bake the assembled Cassoulet for 1 ½ hours at 170°.

To cook in a multifunction oven: Use the setting for fan + grill and cook the duck portions as for a fan oven. Bake the lamb mixture and the assembled Cassoulet on the setting for fan or conventional cooking only as above, switching to fan + grill for the last 15 minutes to make the top especially crusty.

Devilled Pork Chops

To serve 4

Ingredients	Metric	Imperial	American
White breadcrumbs	50 g	2 oz	1 cup
Dried mustard OR	5 ml	1 tsp	1 tsp
Made-up mustard	20 ml	4 tsp	4 tsp
Pork chops or steaks	4	4	4
Egg (optional)	1	1	1

Combine the breadcrumbs with the dried mustard if you are using it. Dip the chops or steaks into the lightly beaten egg and then into the breadcrumbs. Arrange in a single layer in a shallow baking dish.

If you are using made-up mustard, brush it over both sides of the chops or steaks. Use any variety of English, French or whole grain mustard that you like. Do not use the egg, but dip the chops into the crumbs and press gently into both sides. Arrange in a single layer in a shallow baking dish.

To cook conventionally: Bake for ¾–1 hour (according to thickness) at 180° or place the chops on a rack above a roasting pan and grill (broil) on the highest temperature setting for 7–8 minutes on each side or until crisp and brown.
To cook in a fan oven: Bake for 40–50 minutes (according to thickness) at 160° in a shallow dish or 20 minutes at 190° on a rack over a roasting pan. There is no need to turn the meat.
To cook in a multifunction oven: Use the setting for fan + grill and cook for 50 minutes at 160° in a shallow pan or 20 minutes at 190° on a rack over a roasting pan. Turn once.

Variations
Veal chops can be used instead of pork chops, but should not be grilled or cooked on a rack. Dip the chops in egg first, then in crumbs flavoured with either herbs or Parmesan cheese. Omit the mustard.

Use fish fillets instead of meat and proceed as above but do not grill or cook on a rack. The cooking time for fish is less than meat, so watch carefully. Flavour the crumbs with mustard, herbs or cheese.

Substitute slices of streaky (belly) pork (fresh bacon) for the chops. Bake in a shallow dish. The cooking time may be longer than for steaks or chops. When the meat is crisp and brown, drain away the fat and add a tin of baked beans. Cover the dish and bake for 10 minutes longer or until the beans are thoroughly heated.

Quick Pork Casserole

To serve 4

Ingredients	Metric	Imperial	American
Pork cutlets	8	8	8
Chillis (optional)	1–2	1–2	1–2
Clove garlic	1	1	1
Tin tomatoes or	397 g	14 oz	1 lb
Tomato sauce (Passata)			
Sugar	pinch	pinch	pinch
Salt	pinch	pinch	pinch
Dried oregano	5 ml	1 tsp	1 tsp
Bay leaf	1	1	1
Sprig of thyme OR	1	1	1
Dried thyme	5 ml	1 tsp	1 tsp
Red wine (optional)	50 ml	2 fl oz	1/4 cup

Arrange the thinly sliced cutlets in a single layer in an ovenproof dish. Remove the seeds from the chillis if you are using them and chop finely.

Crush the garlic.

Pour all ingredients over the cutlets, cover and bake.

To cook conventionally: Bake for 1 hour at 180°.
To cook in a fan oven: Bake for 50 minutes at 160°.
To cook in a multifunction oven: Use the setting for fan or conventional cooking only and proceed as above.

Variations
Soften the chilli, garlic and a finely chopped onion in 15 ml/ 1 tbsp olive oil before adding to the meat and remaining sauce ingredients. A chopped courgette (zucchini) or green pepper can also be softened with the vegetables.

Quick Chilli

To serve 4

Ingredients	Metric	Imperial	American
Onion	1	1	1
Cloves garlic	2	2	2
Red pepper	1	1	1
Green pepper	1	1	1
Olive oil	30 ml	2 tbsp	2 tbsp
Minced (ground) beef	675 g	1 ½ lb	1 ½ lb
Tinned tomatoes	450 g	1 lb	1 lb
Salt	5 ml	1 tsp	1 tsp
Ground cumin	2 ½ ml	½ tsp	½ tsp
Chilli powder	10 ml	2 tsp	2 tsp
Tinned kidney beans	450 g	1 lb	1 lb
Strong Cheddar cheese (optional)	75 g	3 oz	¾ cup

Soften the finely chopped onion, garlic and peppers in hot oil. If you prefer to use fresh chillis, chop them, remove the seeds and soften with the onion. One chilli makes a mild dish, but use as many as you like to get the right temperature. Extra chilli powder can always be added later if the strength isn't right.

Add the meat and mix well until it loses all its pinkness. Transfer to an overproof dish, add the chopped tomatoes, seasoning and spices, cover and cook.

If you are using uncooked kidney beans, allow 175g/6 oz ½ cup only. Cover with boiling water and leave to soak for 1 hour. Drain well, cover with fresh water and fast boil for 10 minutes, then cook for 1 hour or 15 minutes if you have a pressure cooker. Drain well and add salt to taste. If you are using tinned kidney beans, drain well, rinse and drain again.

Serve the Chilli with tortillas, tacos or rice and accompany with a selection of Mexican jalapeno peppers, shredded lettuce, tomato wedges, chopped raw onion and a salad of grated cucumber mixed with natural yoghurt.

To cook conventionally: Bake the Chilli for 45 minutes at 180°. Add the kidney beans and cook for 10 minutes longer. Remove the lid from the casserole, sprinkle grated cheese on top if you are using it and brown under the grill on its highest temperature setting.
To cook in a fan oven: Bake the Chilli for 45 minutes at 160°. Add the kidney beans and cook for 10 minutes longer. Remove the lid, sprinkle with grated cheese and turn the temperature up to 220°. Bake until the cheese has melted and is beginning to brown.
To cook in a multifunction oven: Use the setting for fan or conventional cooking only and proceed as above. After adding the cheese, turn the temperature to 220° and switch to fan + grill (broiler) until it is golden and bubbling.

Variations

Use stewing steak instead of minced beef and cut into bite-sized cubes. Allow 1 ½ hours for the meat to cook conventionally, or 1 ¼ hours in the fan oven.

Beef Vindaloo

To serve 4

Ingredients	Metric	Imperial	American
Cumin seeds	2 ½ ml	½ tsp	½ tsp
Mustard seeds	2 ½ ml	½ tsp	½ tsp
Black pepper	2 ½ ml	½ tsp	½ tsp
Chilli powder	2 ½ ml	½ tsp	½ tsp
Ground ginger	2 ½ ml	½ tsp	½ tsp
Turmeric	5 ml	1 tsp	1 tsp
White wine vinegar	15 ml	1 tbsp	1 tbsp
Green chilli	1	1	1
Large onion	1	1	1
Cloves garlic	2	2	2
Oil or ghee	50 ml	2 oz	¼ cup
Stewing steak	675 g	1 ½ lb	1 ½ lb
Salt	2 ½ ml	½ tsp	½ tsp

Grind the cumin seeds, mustard seeds and pepper in a mortar and pestle. Add the chilli powder, ground ginger and turmeric. Blend with the vinegar to make a thick paste.

Remove the seeds from the chilli and chop. Brown with the sliced onion and garlic in hot oil or ghee. Stir in the paste and cook for 2–3 minutes.

Place the diced stewing steak in an ovenproof dish. Add the onion and spice mixture, sprinkle with salt and mix well. Cover and cook, stirring occasionally. If the Vindaloo is too dry, add a little water.

To cook conventionally: Bake for 1 ½ hours at 180°.
To cook in a fan oven: Bake for 1 ¼ hours at 160°.
To cook in a multifunction oven: Use the setting for fan or conventional cooking only and proceed as above.

Variation
The 'hotness' of the Vindaloo can be altered by adding more or less chilli powder or more or less fresh chilli. You can also stir some natural yoghurt into the finished Vindaloo to cool it down slightly.

Braised Breast of Veal

To serve 6–8

Ingredients	Metric	Imperial	American
Breast of veal	2–2 ½ kg	4–5 lb	4–5 lb
Salt and pepper			
Flour	30 ml	2 tbsp	2 tbsp
Oil	45 ml	3 tbsp	3 tbsp
Large onion	1	1	1
Carrots	2	2	2
Stick celery	1	1	1
Brown sugar	5 ml	1 tsp	1 tsp
Dry white wine	75 ml	3 fl oz	⅓ cup
Chicken stock	150 ml	5 fl oz	⅔ cup
Stuffing			
Small onion	1	1	1
Stick celery	1	1	1
Margarine	50 g	2 oz	¼ cup
Breadcrumbs	175 g	6 oz	3 cups
Pine kernels	50 g	2 oz	½ cup
(optional)			
Dried oregano	5 ml	1 tsp	1 tsp
Dried basil	5 ml	1 tsp	1 tsp
Sultanas (golden			
raisins)	75 g	3 oz	⅓ cup
Raisins	75 g	3 oz	⅓ cup
Oranges	2	2	2

Bone the veal and either sew the sides leaving a pocket open for the stuffing or flatten slightly so that the stuffing can be spread over the centre and the meat rolled. Shoulder of veal can be used instead of breast.

To prepare the stuffing, soften the finely chopped onion and celery in melted margarine. Stir in all the remaining ingredients, including the finely grated orange rind. Bind with the juice of the oranges. The stuffing should be moist but still crumbly. If it is too crumbly, add a lightly beaten egg. Season to taste with salt and pepper.

Stuff the veal and either fasten the pocket closed with

toothpicks or roll and tie. Dust with seasoned flour and brown on all sides in hot oil. Transfer to an ovenproof dish. Toss the finely chopped vegetables in the remaining oil for 3–4 minutes, sprinkling with brown sugar for the last minute. Spread around the veal. Add the wine and stock to the pan. Bring to the boil, stirring constantly to scrape up any bits clinging to the pan. Pour over the veal and cover.

When the veal is tender, transfer to a warm dish. Strain the sauce and remove as much fat as possible. Boil rapidly to reduce and spoon over the veal. Any meat that is left over can be served cold.

To cook conventionally: Braise the veal for 1 ½ hours at 180° or until the meat feels tender when pierced with a sharp knife.

To cook in a fan oven: Braise the veal for 1 ¼ hours at 160° or until the meat feels tender when pierced with a sharp knife.

To cook in a multifunction oven: Use the setting for fan or conventional cooking only and proceed as above.

(*Illustrated on p. 29*)

Veal Escalopes in Marsala Sauce

To serve 4

Ingredients	Metric	Imperial	American
Veal escalopes	450 g	1 lb	1 lb
Salt and pepper			
Flour	50 g	2 oz	½ cup
Olive oil	30 ml	2 tbsp	2 tbsp
Butter	50 ml	2 oz	¼ cup
Mushrooms	225 g	8 oz	½ lb
Fresh parsley	15 ml	1 tbsp	1 tbsp
Marsala	80 ml	2 ½ fl oz	⅓ cup
Chicken stock	80 ml	2 ½ fl oz	⅓ cup

Pound the veal escalopes between two sheets of greaseproof (waxed) paper until they are as thin as possible. If they are too large to fit in your frying pan (skillet), cut each escalope in half. Dip into seasoned flour.

Heat the olive oil, add the butter and when it has melted, brown the escalopes on both sides. Drain carefully and transfer to an ovenproof dish.

Slice the mushrooms thinly and toss in the remaining oil until soft. Drain well and sprinkle with chopped parsley. Arrange a layer of mushrooms over the veal.

Pour all but 30 ml/2 tbsp fat from the pan. Stir in the Marsala and stock. Bring to the boil, stirring in any bits clinging to the pan. Pour over the veal, cover and bake.

To cook conventionally: Braise the escalopes for 15 minutes at 180°.

To cook in a fan oven: Braise the escalopes for 15 minutes at 160°.

To cook in a multifunction oven: Use the setting for fan or conventional cooking only and proceed as above.

POULTRY & GAME

Chicken with Thyme

To serve 4

Ingredients	Metric	Imperial	American
Onion	1	1	1
Butter	50 g	2 oz	¼ cup
Chicken	1 ½ kg	3 ½ lb	3 ½ lb
Chicken stock	300 ml	½ pt	1 ¼ cups
Dijon mustard	10 ml	2 tsp	2 tsp
White wine vinegar	30 ml	2 tbsp	2 tbsp
Dried thyme OR	5 ml	1 tsp	1 tsp
Fresh thyme	10 ml	2 tsp	2 tsp
Flour	25 g	1 oz	¼ cup
Cheddar cheese	50 g	2 oz	½ cup
Salt and pepper			
Single (light) cream	150 ml	5 fl oz	⅔ cup

Soften the chopped onion in butter. Add the chicken to the pan and colour on all sides. Transfer to an ovenproof casserole.

Combine the chicken stock, mustard, vinegar and thyme. Pour over the chicken, cover and cook as below. When the chicken is cooked, remove from the pan and keep warm.

Stir the pan juices into the flour, stirring constantly to avoid lumps. Return the sauce to the pan and heat, stirring, until thick. Add the grated cheese and stir until melted. Season to taste with salt and freshly ground black pepper. Add the cream and heat gently but do not allow to boil. Spoon some of the sauce over the carved chicken and pass the rest separately.

To cook conventionally: Roast the chicken for 1 ¼ hours at 180°.
To cook in a fan oven: Roast the chicken for 1 hour at 170°.
To cook in a multifunction oven: Use the setting for fan or

conventional cooking only and proceed as above.

Variation
Experiment with different mustard, herbs and cheese.

(Illustrated on p. 17)

Poussin Diablo

To serve 2

Ingredients	Metric	Imperial	American
Poussin (Cornish hens)	2	2	2
Olive oil	30 ml	2 tbsp	2 tbsp
Dried chillis	2–4	2–4	2–4
Sprigs rosemary	2	2	2

Wash the poussin thoroughly inside and out. Pat dry with kitchen towels. Brush all over with olive oil. Sprinkle with crumbled chillis and place a sprig of rosemary inside each one. Arrange on a rack over a roasting pan.

To cook conventionally: Roast the poussin for 45 minutes at 190°. Alternatively, split the poussin in half, sprinkle with chillis and rosemary and brush with olive oil. Grill (broil) on the highest temperature setting for 15 minutes with the skin side down. Turn, brush with oil and grill until the skin is crisp and brown.

To cook in a fan oven: Roast for 45 minutes at 170° if left whole, or 30 minutes if split. If you are splitting the poussin, place skin side up as there will be no need to turn. Prepare as above.

To cook in a multifunction oven: Use the setting for fan only and roast for 45 minutes at 170° if the poussin are whole. If you split the poussin, use the setting for fan + grill, place on the rack skin side up and cook for 30 minutes at 170°. Prepare as above.

Variation
If you cannot get poussin, use the smallest chicken you can find and either split in half or cut into quarters depending on the size. You will have to judge the cooking time by the size of the chicken pieces.

Chicken in Red Wine

To serve 6

Ingredients	Metric	Imperial	American
Rashers (slices) streaky bacon	4	4	4
Olive oil	30 ml	2 tbsp	2 tbsp
Green pepper OR	1	1	1
Sticks celery AND	2	2	2
Carrots	2	2	2
Onion OR	1	1	1
Shallots	4	4	4
Chicken	2 kg	4 ½ lb	4 ½ lb
Brandy	30 ml	2 tbsp	2 tbsp
Tomatoes	225 g	8 oz	½ lb
Red wine	225 ml	8 fl oz	1 cup
Dried thyme OR	5 ml	1 tsp	1 tsp
Fresh thyme	10 ml	2 tsp	2 tsp
Salt and pepper			

Chop the bacon and sauté in 15 ml/1 tbsp hot oil until brown and crisp. Add the finely chopped vegetables and cook gently for 5 minutes or until they begin to soften. Drain well and transfer to an ovenproof dish.

Add the remaining oil to the pan. Cut the chicken into serving pieces and brown well in the hot oil. Drain and arrange on top of the vegetables.

Pour off all but one spoonful of the pan juices. Warm the brandy and add to the pan. Flame. Stir all the brown bits which are clinging to the pan into the brandy. Pour over the chicken.

Plunge the tomatoes into boiling water for 1 minute. Remove from the water, skin, chop and add to the casserole. Pour over the red wine and sprinkle with thyme, salt and pepper. Cover.

To cook conventionally: Bake for 2 hours at 180°, removing the lid for the last 30 minutes.
To cook in a fan oven: Bake for 1 ¾ hours at 160°, removing the lid for the last 20 minutes.

To cook in a multifunction oven: Use the setting for fan or conventional cooking only and proceed as above. After removing the lid, switch to the setting for fan + grill (broiler) for the last 20 minutes.

Duck Fillets with Croutons

To serve 4

Ingredients	Metric	Imperial	American
Duck breasts	2	2	2
Shallots	2	2	2
Clove garlic	1	1	1
Red wine	150 ml	5 fl oz	⅔ cup
Salt and pepper			
Dijon mustard	30 ml	2 tbsp	2 tbsp
Double (heavy) cream	150 ml	5 fl oz	⅔ cup
Slices bread	4	4	4
Chicken liver pâté	125 g	4 oz	¼ lb

Remove the skin from the duck and cut each breast into two. Place on a wire rack over a roasting pan and cook as below.

Sauté the chopped shallot and garlic in 15 ml/1 tbsp duck fat. Add the wine, bring to the boil and simmer for 10 minutes. Season to taste with salt and pepper. Boil rapidly until reduced to half of its original quantity. Strain the sauce, stir in the mustard and cream. Heat through, but do not boil.

To prepare the croutons, spread both sides of each slice of bread with butter, place on a wire rack over a baking tray and cook as below. Spread each crouton with pâté and top with a piece of duck breast. Spoon over the sauce.

To cook conventionally: Roast the duck breast for 15 minutes at 180°. Grill (broil) the croutons as for toast, turning once.

To cook in a fan oven: Roast the duck breast for 15 minutes at 160°. Grill the croutons until golden on 200° but do not turn.

To cook in a multifunction oven: Use the setting for fan + grill. Cook the duck breast for 30 minutes at 160° and grill the croutons at 200°, turning once.

Roast Duck

To serve 2

Ingredients	Metric	Imperial	American
Duck	1 ½ kg	3 ½ lb	3 ½ lb
Salt and pepper			
Orange marmalade or			
honey (optional)	30 ml	2 tbsp	2 tbsp

Wash the duck well inside and out. Pat dry. If possible, hang the duck overnight in a cool room to ensure that it is thoroughly dry. Sprinkle with salt and pepper. Put an onion inside the duck if you like. Prick with a skewer all over to allow the fat to run out while the duck is roasting. Place on a wire rack over a roasting pan. Half an hour before the cooking time is finished, brush the duck with marmalade or honey to help brown the skin.

Serve the duck with either apple sauce or apples browned in butter, a red wine and black cherry sauce or orange slices and watercress. You can also drain off the fat from the roasting pan and stir white wine or cider into the residue in the pan. Reduce the sauce, add some cream and serve separately. This sauce is especially good when flavoured with crushed green peppercorns, Calvados or a little redcurrant jelly.

To cook conventionally: Roast at 180° for 1 ½ hours or until the juices run clear when the leg is pricked with a skewer. If the skin isn't crisp enough, turn the temperature up to 220° for a few minutes to finish off.

To cook in a fan oven: Roast at 170° for 1 ¼ hours or until the juices run clear when the leg is pricked with a skewer. If the skin isn't crisp enough, turn the temperature up to 210° for a few minutes to finish off.

To cook in a multifunction oven: Use the setting for fan only and proceed as above, but finish browning the duck on the fan + grill (broiler) setting.

Variation

Fillets of duck breast can be prepared in a similar way. Place the fillets on a rack over a roasting pan and cook for 30 minutes as above, but use the setting for fan + grill if you have a multifunction oven. Use the pan juices to sauce.

Turkey Breast en Croûte

To serve 4

Ingredients	Metric	Imperial	American
Broccoli or spinach	225 g	8 oz	½ lb
Puff pastry	225 g	8 oz	½ lb
Turkey breast	450 g	1 lb	1 lb
Salt and pepper			
Mozzarella or Gruyère	125 g	4 oz	1 cup
Egg	1	1	1

Cook the broccoli or spinach. Drain well, chop and then leave to cool.

Roll the pastry out as thinly as possible. Cut to make one large or four small rectangles, reserving the trimmings.

Spread the broccoli or spinach over the centre of the pastry leaving ½ cm/¼ inch clear on all sides. Arrange slices of turkey breast over the vegetables and sprinkle with salt and pepper. Sprinkle with sliced or grated cheese. Fold the pastry into the centre to make a neat parcel, sealing the seams well with lightly beaten egg. Place, seam side down, on a lightly greased baking tray. Brush with egg. Use the pastry trimmings to decorate the parcels and brush with egg.

To cook conventionally: Bake for 30 minutes at 200°.
To cook in a fan oven: Bake for 30 minutes at 180°.
To cook in a multifunction oven: Use the setting for fan + bottom and bake for 30 minutes at 180°.

Variations
Substitute chicken breast for turkey.

Use cooked turkey or chicken or a combination of turkey or chicken and ham. Sautéed mushrooms, leeks, cabbage or courgettes (zucchini) can be substituted for the spinach or broccoli.

Rabbit with Mustard Sauce

To serve 4

Ingredients	Metric	Imperial	American
Rabbit	1 ½ kg	3 ½ lb	3 ½ lb
White wine	150 ml	5 fl oz	⅔ cup
Brandy	15 ml	1 tbsp	1 tbsp
White wine vinegar	30 ml	2 tbsp	2 tbsp
Onion	1	1	1
Carrots	2	2	2
Chicken, ham or veal stock	300 ml	½ pt	1 ¼ cups
Butter	25 g	1 oz	2 tbsp
Rashers (slices) streaky bacon	4	4	4
Fresh thyme	5 ml	1 tsp	1 tsp
Clove garlic	1	1	1
Bay leaf	1	1	1
Salt and pepper			
English mustard	10 ml	2 tsp	2 tsp
Double (heavy) cream	150 ml	5 fl oz	⅔ cup

Cut the rabbit into small pieces. Combine the wine, brandy, vinegar, chopped onion and carrots. Add the rabbit pieces, cover and refrigerate overnight, stirring occasionally.

Remove the rabbit from the marinade. Strain the marinade and add to the stock.

Sauté the chopped bacon in butter until crisp. Drain and place in a large casserole. Sauté the rabbit pieces in the remaining butter and bacon fat until they are lightly coloured. Transfer to the casserole. Sprinkle on the thyme, crushed garlic and bay leaf. If you do not have fresh thyme, use 2 ½ ml/½ tsp dried thyme. Add salt and pepper to taste. Pour on the combined stock and marinade. Cover the casserole and bake, adding more stock if necessary while cooking.

When the rabbit is tender, transfer the pieces to an attractive serving dish. Strain the sauce, add the mustard and cream and heat through. Adjust the seasoning if necessary. Pour a little over the rabbit and serve the remainder separately.

To cook conventionally: Bake the casserole for 1 ½ hours at 170°.

To cook in a fan oven: Bake the casserole for 1 ¼ hours at 150°.

To cook in a fan oven: Use the setting for fan or conventional cooking only and proceed as above.

Braised Pheasant with Cider

To serve 4

Ingredients	Metric	Imperial	American
Pheasant	2	2	2
Apples	4	4	4
Flour	75 g	3 oz	¾ cup
Butter	50 g	2 oz	¼ cup
Onions	2	2	2
Stalks celery	2	2	2
Bouquet garni	1	1	1
Stock	225 ml	8 fl oz	1 cup
Cider	225 ml	8 fl oz	1 cup
Salt and pepper			
Double (heavy) cream	150 ml	5 fl oz	⅔ cup

Clean the pheasant well and stuff each with a peeled apple.
Dredge the birds in flour and brown on all sides in melted
butter. Place the pheasant, breast side down, in a large
casserole.

Soften one peeled and chopped apple in the remaining
butter along with the chopped onions and celery. Add to the
casserole with the pheasant and bouquet garni.

Stir 15 g/½ oz/⅛ cup flour into the remaining pan juices.
Slowly add the stock and cider, stirring constantly, until the
sauce thickens. Season with salt and pepper. Pour over the
pheasant. Cover the casserole.

While the pheasant is cooking, slice the remaining apple
and brown in a knob of butter.

Carve the pheasant and arrange on an attractive serving
dish. Strain the sauce and heat through with the cream.
Adjust the seasoning if necessary. Pour some of the sauce
over the pheasant and serve the remainder separately.
Garnish the dish with the sautéed apple slices.

To cook conventionally: Braise for 1 ½ hours at 170°.
To cook in a fan oven: Braise for 1 ¼ hours at 150°.
To cook in a multifunction oven: Use the setting for fan or
conventional cooking only and proceed as above.

Chicken Paprika

To serve 4

Ingredients	Metric	Imperial	American
Chicken	1 ½ kg	3 ½ lb	3 ½ lb
Paprika	10 ml	2 tsp	2 tsp
Salt	2 ½ ml	½ tsp	½ tsp
Red pepper	1	1	1
Green pepper	1	1	1
Onion	1	1	1
Carrots	2	2	2
Mushrooms	125 g	4 oz	¼ lb
Tin tomatoes	397 g	14 oz	1 lb
Sour cream	150 ml	5 fl oz	⅔ cup
Fresh parsley	15 ml	1 tbsp	1 tbsp

Cut the chicken into quarters and rub with paprika and salt.

Cut the peppers into strips. Thinly slice the onions and carrots. Wipe the mushrooms. Arrange all the vegetables in the base of a shallow, ovenproof dish. Place the chicken quarters on top. Pour the juice from the tomatoes over the chicken. Roughly mash the tomatoes and spread over the chicken.

When the chicken is tender, strain the sauce into a pan. Set the vegetables aside but keep warm and return the chicken to the oven so that the skin can brown.

Boil the sauce rapidly until reduced by half. Remove from the heat and stir in the sour cream. Do not boil. Arrange the chicken pieces on a large serving platter and surround with vegetables. Spoon some sauce over the chicken, garnish with parsley and serve the rest of the sauce separately.

To cook conventionally: Bake the chicken for 50 minutes at 180°. After straining off the sauce, place under the grill (broiler) at the highest temperature setting for 5 minutes.
To cook in a fan oven: Bake the chicken for 45 minutes at 160°. Return to the oven at 190° so that the skin can brown.
To cook in a multifunction oven: Use fan or conventional cooking setting only and bake for 45 minutes at 160°. Return to oven on fan + grill setting to brown skin.

FISH AND SEAFOOD

Haddock Provençal

To serve 4

Ingredients	Metric	Imperial	American
Cloves garlic	2	2	2
Red or green pepper	1	1	1
Onion	1	1	1
Mushrooms	125 g	4 oz	¼ lb
Olive oil	75 ml	5 tbsp	⅓ cup
Haddock	675 g	1 ½ lb	1 ½ lb
Flour	75 ml	5 tbsp	5 tbsp
Salt and black or cayenne pepper			
Brandy	60 ml	4 tbsp	4 tbsp
Tomatoes	4	4	4
Tomato purée	5 ml	1 tsp	1 tsp
Sugar	pinch	pinch	pinch
Thyme	pinch	pinch	pinch
Bay leaf	1	1	1
White wine	120 ml	4 fl oz	½ cup

Finely chop the garlic, pepper, onion and mushrooms. Soften in hot oil.

Skin the fish and cut into bite-sized pieces. Combine the flour, salt and pepper. Toss the fish in the flour. Add the fish to the vegetables and cook, stirring constantly, until sealed.

Warm the brandy, pour over the fish and set alight. When the flames have died down, transfer the fish and vegetables to an ovenproof dish.

Plunge the tomatoes into boiling water then remove, skin and chop. Add to the fish along with the remaining ingredients. Cover.

To cook conventionally: Bake for 30 minutes at 180°.

To cook in a fan oven: Bake for 30 minutes at 160°.
To cook in a multifunction oven: Use the setting for fan or conventional cooking only and proceed as above.

Variation
Substitute monkfish, turbot or halibut for the haddock. A few prawns (shrimp) can be added at the last minute as a garnish.

Monkfish en Papillote

To serve 4

Ingredients	Metric	Imperial	American
Monkfish tail	900 g	2 lb	2 lb
Cloves garlic	4	4	4
Fresh parsley	30 ml	2 tbsp	2 tbsp
Butter	25 g	1 oz	2 tbsp
Dry white wine	50 ml	2 fl oz	¼ cup
Sauce			
Shallot OR	1	1	1
Onion	15 ml	1 tbsp	1 tbsp
Butter	15 g	½ oz	1 tbsp
Dry white wine	150 ml	5 fl oz	⅔ cup
Salt and pepper			

Remove the skin from the monkfish and place in the centre of a large square of kitchen foil. Sprinkle with crushed garlic and chopped parsley. Dot with butter. Pour over the wine and close the parcel securely.

While the monkfish is baking, soften the finely chopped shallot or onion in butter. Add the wine and boil rapidly until the sauce has reduced to just 45 ml/3 tbsp.

Remove the monkfish from its foil and keep warm on a serving dish. Add the juice to the sauce, season to taste and pour over the fish. Garnish with more fresh parsley.

To cook conventionally: Bake for 1 hour at 180°.
To cook in a fan oven: Bake for 50 minutes at 170°.
To cook in a multifunction oven: Use the setting for fan or conventional cooking only and proceed as above.

Variations
Use large prawns (shrimp) or scallops instead of monkfish and cook for 10–15 minutes only. Alternatively, prawns, scallops, squid or a mixture of these with or without monkfish pieces can be used. The fish can also be arranged in a shallow ovenproof dish and grilled in a conventional or fan oven for 10–15 minutes at 210°. If you have a multifunction oven, use the setting for fan + grill (broiler).

Stuffed Mussels

To serve 4

Ingredients	Metric	Imperial	American
Mussels	900 g	2 lb	2 lb
Dry white wine	150 ml	5 fl oz	⅔ cup
Butter	125 g	4 oz	½ cup
Cloves garlic	2	2	2
Fresh parsley	30 ml	2 tbsp	2 tbsp
White breadcrumbs	15 ml	1 tbsp	1 tbsp
Gruyère cheese	30 ml	2 tbsp	2 tbsp

Scrub the mussels and place in a large pan with the wine. There should be only a single layer of mussels in the pan, so you may have to cook more than one batch. Cover the pan and cook over a high flame, shaking the pan occasionally, until the shells open, approximately 3–4 minutes. Remove the mussels from the pan immediately. Discard half of each shell. Arrange the mussels in a single layer in an ovenproof dish.

Combine the butter, crushed garlic and chopped parsley. Place a knob of this butter on each mussel. Sprinkle with the combined breadcrumbs and grated cheese.

To cook conventionally: Bake for 10 minutes at 180°.
To cook in a fan oven: Bake for 10 minutes at 160°.
To cook in a multifunction oven: Use the setting for fan + grill (broiler). Bake the mussels for 10 minutes at 160°.

Variations
Omit the cheese and use any combination of breadcrumbs, herbs and garlic you like to make the stuffing. You can also soften an onion and/or chopped mushroom stems in butter to mix with the crumbs. Moisten if necessary with a spoonful of the wine in which the mussels were cooked. Try adding chopped spinach and Tabasco sauce (hot pepper sauce) to the stuffing for extra variety.

Clams or oysters can be used instead of mussels. The stuffing is also delicious when used with large mushroom caps.

Stuffed Plaice

To serve 4

Ingredients	Metric	Imperial	American
Leeks	3	3	3
Carrots	3	3	3
Butter	75 g	3 oz	6 tbsp
Salt and pepper			
Fresh ginger	5 ml	1 tsp	1 tsp
Cloves garlic	2	2	2
Crabmeat	225 g	8 oz	1 cup
Tomato purée	10 ml	2 tsp	2 tsp
Single (light) cream	150 ml	5 fl oz	⅔ cup
Plaice (flounder) fillets	8	8	8
Dry white wine	120 ml	4 fl oz	½ cup

Sweat the finely chopped leeks and carrots in 50 g/2 oz/¼ cup butter for 5 minutes. Spread over the base of a shallow ovenproof dish. Season to taste with salt and freshly ground black pepper.

Soften the finely chopped ginger and garlic in the remaining butter. Stir in the crabmeat and mix well. Add the tomato purée and 50 ml/2 fl oz/¼ cup cream. Stir until well blended and thoroughly warm. Spread the mixture over the plaice fillets, roll up and arrange in a single layer on the bed of vegetables. Season with salt and pepper. Pour over the wine and cover with foil.

When the fish is cooked, strain off the pan juices and heat very gently with the remaining cream. Do not boil. Season to taste, pour over the fish and serve immediately.

To cook conventionally: Bake for 30 minutes at 180°.
To cook in a fan oven: Bake for 30 minutes at 160°.
To cook in a multifunction oven: Use the setting for fan or conventional cooking only and proceed as above.

Variations

Substitute fillets of sole for plaice.

Stuff the fish with softened mushrooms and shallots mixed with prawns (shrimp) instead of crabmeat and use Marsala instead of white wine.

Substitute courgettes (zucchini), celeriac, fennel or chicory (endive) for the leeks and carrots. Cut into thin, julienne strips rather than chop. Any combination of vegetables in season can be used, but undercook them slightly so that they are still crunchy.

Cod with Sour Cream Sauce

To serve 4

Ingredients	Metric	Imperial	American
Cod steaks or fillets	4	4	4
Milk	120 ml	4 fl oz	½ cup
Fresh spinach	450 g	1 lb	1 lb
Salt and pepper			
Potatoes	450 g	1 lb	1 lb
Butter	50 g	2 oz	¼ cup
Onion	1	1	1
Mushrooms	125 g	4 oz	1 cup
Sour cream	300 ml	½ pint	1 ¼ cups
Lemon juice	40 ml	2 ½ tbsp	2 ½ tbsp
White wine vinegar	15 ml	1 tbsp	1 tbsp
Paprika	pinch	pinch	pinch

Place the cod steaks or fillets in a shallow ovenproof dish and pour over the milk. Cover and bake until the fish flakes easily. Remove from the pan and set aside.

Cook the spinach, drain well and place in the bottom of one large or four individual ovenproof dishes. Place the fish on top of the spinach. Season to taste with salt and pepper.

Boil the potatoes, drain well and mash with 25 g/1 oz/2 tbsp butter and a little milk. Season well.

Soften the finely chopped onion and sliced mushrooms in the remaining butter. Stir in the sour cream, lemon juice, vinegar and paprika. Season to taste. Spoon the sauce over the fish. Pipe the mashed potatoes around the dish edge.

To cook conventionally: Poach the cod for 20–25 minutes at 180°. Bake the assembled dish for 10 minutes at 210° or until the potatoes are golden and the sauce bubbling.

To cook in a fan oven: Poach the cod for 15–20 minutes at 160°. Bake the assembled dish for 10 minutes at 200° or until the potatoes are golden and the sauce bubbling.

To cook in a multifunction oven: Poach the cod on the setting for fan or conventional cooking only as above. Bake the assembled dish for 10 minutes at 200° on the setting for fan + grill (broiler).

Variation

Substitute haddock, halibut, whiting or any other white fish that is available for the cod. The spinach can be omitted or replaced with broccoli or cauliflower.

Grilled Mullet

To serve 4

Ingredients	Metric	Imperial	American
Red mullet	4	4	4
Salt and pepper			
Olive oil	15 ml	1 tbsp	1 tbsp
Red wine	45 ml	3 tbsp	3 tbsp
Fresh thyme	sprig	sprig	sprig
Fresh fennel	sprig	sprig	sprig

Clean the fish, but do not remove the liver. Make 2–3 cuts on each side. Season with salt and pepper.

Combine the oil, wine and herbs. If you do not have fresh herbs, use a pinch each of dried thyme and fennel. Turn the fish in the marinade until well covered and refrigerate for 2 hours, turning occasionally. Remove the mullet from the marinade and arrange on a rack over a roasting pan.

To cook conventionally: Grill (broil) the mullet on the highest temperature setting for 8–10 minutes on each side.
To cook in a fan oven: Grill the mullet for 15–20 minutes according to size at 210°. There is no need to turn.
To cook in a multifunction oven: Use the setting for fan + grill and cook the mullet for 15–20 minutes at 210°. Turn once.

Variations

The red wine in the marinade can be replaced by lemon juice and the herbs varied according to taste and availability.

Use whole bulb fennel instead of herbs. Slice and blanch in boiling water for 5 minutes then sauté with a chopped onion in butter for 5 minutes. Place in a shallow ovenproof dish, top with the cleaned and seasoned mullet, and bake for 20–30 minutes at 180° in a conventional oven or 160° in a fan oven. If you have a multifunction oven, use the setting for fan only.

Stuffed Trout

To serve 4

Ingredients	Metric	Imperial	American
Trout	4	4	4
Salt and pepper			
Carrots	2	2	2
Sticks celery	2	2	2
Small courgettes (zucchini)	2	2	2
Mushrooms	50 g	2 oz	½ cup
Butter	25 g	1 oz	2 tbsp
Dry sherry or vermouth	50 ml	2 fl oz	¼ cup
Fresh herbs	15 ml	1 tbsp	1 tbsp

Clean and bone the trout. Season inside and out with salt and pepper. Arrange each trout on a large square of buttered foil.

Sauté the finely chopped vegetables in melted butter for 2–3 minutes. Season with salt and pepper. Add the sherry or vermouth and herbs (try parsley, basil or tarragon). Bring to the boil, and simmer for 5 minutes. Cool slightly, then stuff the trout and seal the foil parcel.

To cook conventionally: Bake for 20 minutes at 200°.
To cook in a fan oven: Bake for 20 minutes at 180°.
To cook in a multifunction oven: Use the setting for fan or conventional cooking only and proceed as above.

Variations

For a more filling meal, add 30 ml/2 tbsp breadcrumbs to the vegetables before stuffing the trout.

Soften the vegetables and arrange in a shallow ovenproof dish. Season the trout with salt, pepper and lemon juice. Place on the bed of vegetables, cover and bake as above. For a special occasion, stir 150 ml/5 fl oz/⅔ cup single (light) cream into the pan juices after the trout is cooked.

Any other vegetables you have available can be substituted for those above — leeks and fennel are particularly good with trout.

Monkfish Kebabs

To serve 4

Ingredients	Metric	Imperial	American
Lemon juice	30 ml	2 tbsp	2 tbsp
Olive oil	30 ml	2 tbsp	2 tbsp
Onion	30 ml	2 tbsp	2 tbsp
Paprika	5 ml	1 tsp	1 tsp
Salt	5 ml	1 tsp	1 tsp
Monkfish	900 g	2 lb	2 lb
Mushrooms	8	8	8
Tomatoes	4	4	4
Bay leaves	4	4	4
Pepper	1	1	1
Spanish onion OR	1	1	1
baby onions	8	8	8
Courgettes (zucchini)	4	4	4

Whisk the lemon juice into the oil. Using a garlic press, squeeze the onion and add the juice to the oil and lemon juice. Stir in the paprika and salt.

Remove the skin from the monkfish and cut into 2 ½ cm/ 1 inch cubes. Add to the marinade, mix well, cover and refrigerate for 2 hours, stirring occasionally.

Assemble the kebabs by alternating pieces of fish with mushrooms, tomato halves, a bay leaf, and chunks of pepper (red, yellow or green as available), Spanish onion and courgettes on skewers. Arrange on a rack over a grill (broiler) pan and brush with any remaining marinade.

To cook conventionally: Grill (broil) on the highest temperature setting, turning frequently until the fish is firm and the vegetables tender.
To cook in a fan oven: Grill on 210° for approximately 10 minutes or until the fish is firm and the vegetables are tender. There is no need to turn.

(Illustrated on p. 33)

Grilled Trout Steaks

To serve 4

Ingredients	Metric	Imperial	American
Trout steaks	4	4	4
Orange	1	1	1
Shallot	1	1	1
White wine vinegar	60 ml	4 tbsp	4 tbsp
Fresh thyme	15 ml	1 tbsp	1 tbsp
Salt and pepper			

Cut the trout steaks so that they are approximately 5 cm/
2 inches thick. Add the grated orange rind, orange juice and
finely chopped shallot to the wine vinegar and mix well. Add
the thyme and season to taste. If you cannot get fresh thyme,
use 10 ml/2 tsp dried thyme or any other herb that you prefer.
Turn the trout steaks in the marinade. Cover and refrigerate
for 2 hours, turning occasionally.

Arrange the trout steaks on a rack over a roasting pan.
When cooked, serve garnished with orange slices.

To cook conventionally: Grill (broil) on the highest
temperature setting for 5–10 minutes on each side.
To cook in a fan oven: Grill at 220° for 15–20 minutes or until
the steaks are firm to the touch. Do not turn.
To cook in a multifunction oven: Use the setting for fan +
grill. Cook the trout at 220° for 5 minutes on each side.

Variations

Stir a few spoonfuls of thick yoghurt, double (heavy) or sour
cream into the pan juices and pour over the trout.

Marinate the trout in 15 ml/1 tbsp oil mixed with 15 ml/1
tbsp crushed green peppercorns instead of the mixture above.

Use salmon, halibut or swordfish steaks instead of trout.

DESSERTS AND PUDDINGS

Baked Bananas

To serve 4

Ingredients	Metric	Imperial	American
Bananas	4	4	4
Rum	60 ml	4 tbsp	4 tbsp
Butter	20 ml	4 tsp	4 tsp
Brown sugar	20 ml	4 tsp	4 tsp
Lime juice	20 ml	4 tsp	4 tsp
Mixed spice	pinch	pinch	pinch

Peel the bananas and place each one on a square of kitchen foil. Pour over the rum, dot with butter and brown sugar, sprinkle with lime juice and mixed spice. Seal the parcels and place on a baking tray.

Serve the bananas hot with double (heavy) cream or ice cream.

To cook conventionally: Bake for 10–15 minutes at 200°.
To cook in a fan oven: Bake for 10–15 minutes at 180°.
To cook in a multifunction oven: Use the setting for fan or conventional cooking only and proceed as above.

Variations

Use pineapple rings or quarters of a whole, fresh pineapple, instead of the bananas. The pineapple will need up to 30 minutes cooking time according to its thickness.

Lemon juice can be substituted for lime juice.

Cointreau or Curaçao can be substituted for rum. If you are baking pineapple, use Kirsch for the liqueur.

As a children's treat, sprinkle the bananas with chopped or grated chocolate and a knob of butter before baking. Omit all the other ingredients.

Baked Alaska

To serve 8–10

Ingredients	Metric	Imperial	American
Eggs	3	3	3
Caster sugar	225 g	8 oz	1 cup
Plain (all-purpose) flour	75 g	3 oz	¾ cup
Liqueur	45 ml	3 tbsp	3 tbsp
Fruit	125 g	4 oz	¼ lb
Ice cream	1 litre	2 pints	2 ½ pints
Egg whites	4	4	4
Cream of tartar	pinch	pinch	pinch
Icing (confectioners') sugar	45 ml	3 tbsp	3 tbsp

Whisk the eggs and half of the caster sugar together until very thick and light. The mixture should retain the impression of the whisk for a few seconds after it is removed. Carefully sieve half of the flour into the eggs and fold in gently. Fold in the remaining flour. Pour the batter into a greased and lined tin — either a Swiss roll tin (jelly roll pan) if you want a thin base, or a 20 cm/8 inch square or round tin (pan).

When the cake has cooled, sprinkle with the liqueur of your choice and arrange the fruit on top leaving 1 cm/½ inch clear on all sides. The fruit and liqueur can be anything you like — berries, pineapple, peaches or a mixture for example combined with Kirsch, Cointreau or rum.

Freeze the ice cream in a mould the same size and shape as the sponge base but 1 cm/½ inch smaller all around. Be sure that the ice cream is very solid.

Whisk the egg whites with the cream of tartar until they are stiff but not dry. Gradually add the remaining caster sugar, whisking constantly until the meringue is stiff again. Spoon or pipe over the ice cream, ensuring that the cake and ice cream are completely sealed. Sprinkle with sieved icing sugar.

To cook conventionally: Bake the sponge for 15 minutes at 180°. Brown the assembled dessert under the highest grill (broiler) setting for 5 minutes or until golden.

To cook in a fan oven: Bake the sponge for 15 minutes at 170°. Brown the assembled dessert at 210° for 5 minutes or until golden.

To cook in a multifunction oven: Use the setting for fan or conventional cooking only and bake the sponge as above. Use the setting for fan + grill (broiler) for the assembled dessert and bake for 5 minutes at 210° or until golden.

Variation

Flavour the sponge batter with 15 ml/1 tbsp sieved cocoa. Omit the fruit, sprinkle the base with Kahlua or Tia Maria and top with coffee, chocolate, almond or pecan ice cream. Finish the Baked Alaska as above.

Strawberry Shortcake

To serve 8

Ingredients	Metric	Imperial	American
Fresh strawberries	450 g	1 lb	1 lb
Sugar	50 g	2 oz	¼ cup
Plain (all-purpose) flour	225 g	8 oz	2 cups
Baking powder	20 ml	4 tsp	4 tsp
Salt	2 ½ ml	½ tsp	½ tsp
Sugar	15 ml	1 tbsp	1 tbsp
Unsalted butter	75 g	3 oz	6 tbsp
Milk	120 ml	4 fl oz	½ cup
Double (heavy) cream	300 ml	½ pint	1 ¼ cups

Set aside eight strawberries to decorate the shortcake and slice the remainder. Sprinkle with sugar and refrigerate for 1 hour.

Sieve the flour and baking powder. Stir in the salt and sugar.

Rub in 50 g/2 oz/4 tbsp of butter until the mixture resembles coarse breadcrumbs. Bind with the milk to make a firm dough. Roll out to make a thick circle, approximately 23 cm/9 inches in diameter. Place on a greased baking tray.

When the shortcake has baked and cooled, slice in half to make two layers. Place the bottom layer on an attractive serving dish. Brush with the remaining, melted butter.

Whisk the cream until it is thick and beginning to hold its shape. Spread ¾ of the cream over the bottom layer of shortcake. Arrange the sliced strawberries on top and cover with the second layer of shortcake.

Decorate with the remaining cream and the reserved strawberries, either whole or sliced in half. Serve as soon as possible after assembling.

To cook conventionally: Bake the shortcake for 10–15 minutes at 210°.

To cook in a fan oven: Bake the shortcake for 10–15 minutes at 200°.

To cook in a multifunction oven: Use the setting for fan + bottom. Bake the shortcake for 10–15 minutes at 200°.

Variations

Substitute raspberries,blackberries, blueberries, peaches, pineapple or a combination of fruits for the strawberries.

Cut the shortcake dough into eight pieces, roll out and bake as above but assemble individual shortcakes.

(Illustrated on p. 9)

Lemon Layer Pudding

To serve 4

Ingredients	Metric	Imperial	American
Butter or margarine	50 g	2 oz	¼ cup
Sugar	75 g	3 oz	⅓ cup
Lemons	2	2	2
Eggs, separated	2	2	2
Self-raising (self-rising) flour	50 g	2 oz	½ cup
Milk	150 ml	5 fl oz	⅔ cup

Beat the butter or margarine with the sugar and finely grated lemon rind until the mixture is soft and well blended. Add the egg yolks and mix well. Add the flour and milk alternately, mixing well after each addition.

Whisk the egg whites until they are stiff but not dry. Gently fold into the batter, starting with just one spoonful and gradually adding the remainder. Pour into a well greased pie dish or 900 ml/1 ½ pt/2 pt casserole.

The pudding can be served either hot or cold.

To cook conventionally: Bake for 30 minutes at 180°.
To cook in a fan oven: Bake for 30 minutes at 160°.
To cook in a multifunction oven: Use the setting for fan or conventional cooking only and proceed as above.

(Illustrated on p. 29)

Walnut Meringue Torte

Tc serve 8–10

Ingredients	Metric	Imperial	American
Egg whites	4	4	4
Caster sugar	225g	8 oz	1 cup
Ground walnuts	50 g	2 oz	½ cup
Ice cream OR	575 ml	1 pint	2 ½ cups
Poached fruit	450 g	1 lb	2 cups
Double (heavy) cream	225 ml	8 fl oz	1 cup
Sugar	125 g	4 oz	½ cup
Walnut halves	16	16	16

Whisk the egg whites until they are stiff but not dry. Add the sugar, one spoonful at a time, and continue whisking until the meringue is stiff again. Gently fold in the ground nuts. Spoon carefully into a piping (pastry) bag.

Line two baking trays with greaseproof (waxed) paper. Trace a 23 cm/9 inch circle on each. On the first tray, pipe the meringue in concentric circles to fill the shape. Smooth gently with a palette knife. On the second tray, pipe one ring of meringue around the outside of the circle. Pipe three parallel lines in each direction to form a lattice.

When the meringues have baked and cooled, carefully remove the greaseproof paper. Place the meringue circle on an attractive serving dish.

If you are using ice cream, freeze it in a 23 cm/9 inch round tin until it is very firm. Remove from the tin when you are ready to assemble the Torte and carefully place on the meringue circle. Alternatively, arrange a layer of sliced, poached fruit (cooked in either sugar syrup, wine or apple juice) on the meringue base. Any fruit you like can be used — try plums, mango, pineapple, apricots or a combination of either fresh or dried fruits to make a compote.

Whisk the cream until it is thick and just beginning to hold its shape. Spread over the ice cream or fruit. Top with the meringue lattice, pressing down gently so that the cream oozes through the gaps.

Melt the sugar over a very low heat in a heavy bottomed pan.

Stir constantly, until the sugar has melted and turned golden. Add the walnut halves and stir until they are well coated in sugar. Remove the nuts from the pan and place on a sheet of greaseproof (waxed) paper for a few minutes or until the sugar has dried. Place one walnut half in each of the gaps in the lattice.

Serve the Walnut Meringue Torte as soon as possible after assembling.

To cook conventionally: Bake the meringues for 30 minutes at 140°.

To cook in a fan oven: Bake the meringues for 30 minutes at 130°.

To cook in a multifunction oven: Use the setting for fan or conventional cooking only and proceed as above.

PASTRY

Cheese en Croûte

To serve 8–12

Ingredients	Metric	Imperial	American
Puff pastry or	450 g	1 lb	1 lb
Brioche dough			
Brie OR	1	1	1
Camembert wedges	4	4	4
Egg	1	1	1

Roll the pastry out until it is as thin as possible. If you are using Camembert, the pastry should be divided into four pieces before you roll it out. Cut into a circle that is 2 ½ cm/1 inch larger than the cheese all around. Save the pastry trimmings.

Place the cheese in the centre of the pastry and fold the edges up over the top. Brush the edges of the pastry with lightly beaten egg.

Roll the pastry trimmings to make a circle or small circles for Camembert. Place on top of the cheese and seal well. Trim carefully and use any leftover pieces to cut into leaves, diamonds, etc. to decorate the top. Glaze with beaten egg and place on a greased baking sheet.

When the cheese has been baked, leave to rest for 15 minutes before serving garnished with either a salad or a purée of red fruit, for example redcurrants, cranberries or raspberries.

To cook conventionally: Bake at 180° for 15–20 minutes or until the pastry is well risen and golden.
To cook in a fan oven: Bake at 170° for 15–20 minutes or until the pastry is well risen and golden.
To cook in a multifunction oven: Use the setting for fan + bottom. Bake at 210° for 25 minutes or until the pastry is well risen and golden.

Variations

Spread the base of the pastry with a thin layer of redcurrant jelly or raspberry purée before wrapping the cheese.

Use puff pastry to make vol au vent cases 8 cm/3 inches larger than the cheese. Bake for 15 minutes at 200° in a conventional oven or 180° in a fan oven. Place the cheese in the vols au vent, sprinkle with flaked almonds and heat through for 15 minutes at 200° in a conventional oven or 180° in a fan oven so that the cheese melts and the almonds toast. If you have a multifunction oven, use the setting for fan + bottom to bake the vols au vent then switch to fan + top to heat the cheese.

Phyllo (filo) pastry, shortcrust or a cream cheese pastry bound with egg yolk can be used instead of puff pastry or brioche dough. Phyllo should be glazed with melted butter rather than beaten egg.

Substitute crumbled Feta cheese mixed with dill seeds, egg yolk, butter and freshly ground black pepper. Cream cheese mixed with melted butter, crushed garlic and fresh herbs is also delicious.

Turkey and Cranberry-Pie

To serve 6–8

Ingredients	Metric	Imperial	American
Pastry			
Plain flour	225 g	8 oz	2 cups
Small egg	1	1	1
Butter	150 g	5 oz	⅔ cup
Salt	2 ½ ml	½ tsp	½ tsp
Sugar	15 ml	1 tbsp	1 tbsp
Water	50 ml	2 fl oz	¼ cup
Filling			
Cooked turkey	300 g	10 oz	1 ¼ cups
Cooked ham	175 g	6 oz	¾ cup
Cranberry sauce	125 g	4 oz	½ cup
Black pepper			
Egg	1	1	1
Chicken stock	150 ml	5 fl oz	⅔ cup

Sieve the flour into a large mixing bowl and make a well in the centre. Break the egg into the well, add the diced butter, salt, sugar and water. Gradually draw the flour into the centre to form a dough. Mix well and then knead until smooth. (This can be done with an electric mixer or food processor if you have one.) Wrap in clingfilm and chill for 2 hours.

Cut the pastry into two pieces, one twice the size of the other. Roll out the larger piece and use to line the base and sides of a 20 cm/8 inch loose-bottomed cake tin. Fill with a layer of diced turkey and ham, top with cranberry sauce and finish with the remaining turkey and ham. Season with pepper.

Roll out the remaining piece of pastry and place over the top of the pie, sealing well with beaten egg. Use any trimmings to decorate the top of the pie and glaze once more with egg. Make a hole in the top crust so that the steam can escape and insert a pastry funnel or a small roll of cardboard to ensure that the hole doesn't close while the pie is baking.

While the pie is in the oven, boil the chicken stock until it reduces to just a few spoonfuls. Slowly pour the stock into the baked pie through the top hole and leave to cool.

To cook conventionally: Bake the pie at 180° for 35 minutes or until the pastry is crisp and golden.
To cook in a fan oven: Bake the pie at 160° for 35 minutes or until the pastry is crisp and golden.

To cook in a multifunction oven: Use the setting for fan + bottom. Bake the pie at 160° for 50 minutes or until the pastry is crisp and golden.

Raspberry Coconut Tart

To serve 6–8

Ingredients	Metric	Imperial	American
Base			
Butter	50 g	2 oz	1/4 cup
Margarine	50 g	2 oz	1/4 cup
Plain (all-purpose) flour	175 g	6 oz	1 1/2 cups
Egg	1	1	1
Filling			
Raspberry jam	60 ml	4 tbsp	4 tbsp
Soft margarine	125 g	4 oz	1/2 cup
Sugar	75 g	3 oz	1/3 cup
Plain (all-purpose) flour	125 g	4 oz	1 cup
Baking powder	5 ml	1 tsp	1 tsp
Eggs	2	2	2
Almond essence (extract)	5 ml	1 tsp	1 tsp
Desiccated (shredded) coconut	50 g	2 oz	2/3 cup

Rub the butter and margarine into the flour for the pastry base until the mixture resembles coarse breadcrumbs. Bind with the lightly beaten egg to make a dough. If necessary, add a few drops of water. Wrap in clingfilm and chill for 1 hour. Roll out the pastry and line the base and sides of a 20 cm/8 inch loose-bottomed sandwich tin.

When the pastry is baked, cool slightly and then spread with raspberry jam.

To prepare the filling, beat the soft margarine with the sugar, flour and baking powder until smooth. Add the eggs and almond essence. Mix well. Stir in the coconut and carefully spoon over the jam in the pastry case.

To cook conventionally: Pre-heat the oven. Bake the pastry case for 10 minutes at 220°. Bake the filled tart for 30 minutes at 180°.

To cook in a fan oven: Pre-heat the oven. Bake the pastry case for 5 minutes at 220°. Bake the filled tart for 30 minutes at 170°.

To cook in a multifunction oven: Pre-heat the oven. Use the setting for fan + base and bake the pastry case for 5 minutes at 220°. Change to the setting for fan only and bake the filled tart for 30 minutes at 170°.

Chocolate Cream Pie

To serve 8

Ingredients	Metric	Imperial	American
Base			
Unsalted butter	175 g	6 oz	¾ cup
Caster sugar	75 g	3 oz	⅓ cup
Plain (all-purpose) flour	175 g	6 oz	1 ½ cups
Cornflour (cornstarch)	50 g	2 oz	¼ cup
Filling			
Plain (semi-sweet) chocolate	50 g	2 oz	¼ cup
Cointreau	15 ml	1 tbsp	1 tbsp
Single (light) cream	300 ml	½ pt	1 ¼ cups
Cornflour (cornstarch)	30 ml	2 tbsp	2 tbsp
Caster sugar	225 g	8 oz	1 cup
Eggs	2	2	2
Unsalted butter	50 g	2 oz	¼ cup
Topping			
Double (heavy) cream	150 ml	5 fl oz	⅔ cup
Cointreau	15 ml	1 tbsp	1 tbsp
Melted chocolate	5 ml	1 tsp	1 tsp

Cream the butter and sugar for the base until very light and fluffy. Carefully fold in the combined flour and cornflour. Mix until you have a stiff dough. Gently press onto the base and up the sides of a 25 cm/10 inch loose-bottomed flan tin. Prick with a fork to prevent bubbles forming.

While the base is baking and cooling, melt the chocolate with the Cointreau for the filling in a bowl over a pan of simmering water. Stir in the combined cream, cornflour and sugar. Start with just one spoonful and gradually add the remainder. Use vanilla-flavoured caster sugar if you have have some.

Stir the lightly beaten eggs into the chocolate and cook, stirring constantly, over a very low heat until thick and smooth. Remove from the heat and stir in the diced butter. When the filling has cooled, pour over the base of the pie and chill for 2 hours or longer.

Whisk the double cream with the Cointreau until it is just stiff enough to hold its shape. Spoon or pipe over the pie. Drizzle melted chocolate on top to make an attractive pattern.

To cook conventionally: Bake the pie base for 25 minutes at 180°.
To cook in a fan oven: Bake the pie base for 25 minutes at 160°.
To cook in a multifunction oven: Use the setting for fan or conventional cooking only and proceed as above.

Strudel

To serve 8–10

Ingredients	Metric	Imperial	American
Strong flour	225 g	8 oz	2 cups
Small egg	1	1	1
Sugar	5 ml	1 tsp	1 tsp
Salt	pinch	pinch	pinch
Melted butter	125 g	4 oz	½ cup
Warm water	50 ml	2 fl oz	¼ cup

Pour the flour onto a clean work surface or into a large bowl and make a well in the middle. Break the egg into the well and sprinkle with sugar, salt and 15 ml/1 tbsp butter. Gradually draw the flour into the centre of the well, mixing with your hands to make a dough. Add the water a little at a time to make a soft, sticky dough. Knead until smooth and elastic. (The dough can be made in an electric mixer or food processor if you have one.) Cover and leave to rest for 30 minutes.

Spread a clean table cloth or sheet over a large table or work surface. Sprinkle with flour and roll the dough out to make a large circle. Lightly brush the dough with melted butter. Place your hands under the dough, palms down. Slowly rotate the circle, lifting and stretching a small section at a time until the pastry is very thin and nearly transparent. This takes a great deal of care and practice, so be patient. Trim off the edges if they are thick or hard.

Brush the centre of the pastry with melted butter, leaving 2 ½ cm/1 inch clear on all sides. Spread with your favourite filling — cherry, apple, cheese or a savoury mixture of fish, vegetables or chicken. Fold the top, bottom and one long side of the pastry over the filling. Brush the fourth side with melted butter and slip a sheet of greaseproof paper (waxed) under it. Gently roll the strudel, using the cloth to help, from the folded edge towards the unfolded edge. You should finish with a complete roll, seam side down, on the greaseproof paper. Carefully transfer to a greased baking tray. If the strudel is too large for your tray, curve the ends in to make a crescent shape. Brush with melted butter. If the top browns too quickly, cover with greaseproof paper.

To cook conventionally: Bake the strudel at 190° for 30 minutes or until crisp and golden.
To cook in a fan oven: Bake the strudel at 170° for 30 minutes or until crisp and golden.
To cook in a multifunction oven: Use the setting for fan + bottom. Bake the strudel at 170° for 30 minutes or until crisp and golden.

Cream Puffs

To make 36

Ingredients	Metric	Imperial	American
Choux Pastry			
Plain (all-purpose) flour	65 g	2 ½ oz	⅔ cup
Salt	pinch	pinch	pinch
Water	150 ml	5 fl oz	⅔ cup
Butter	50 g	2 oz	¼ cup
Eggs	2	2	2
Filling			
Sugar	45 ml	3 tbsp	3 tbsp
Cornflour (cornstarch)	10 ml	2 tsp	2 tsp
Flour	15 ml	1 tbsp	1 tbsp
Egg	1	1	1
Egg yolk	1	1	1
Milk	300 ml	½ pt	1 ¼ cups
Icing (confectioners') sugar	45 ml	3 tbsp	3 tbsp

Sieve the flour for the choux pastry and mix with the salt.

Heat the water with the butter until the butter has melted and the water is just about to boil. Add the flour and stir until the mixture forms a ball which leaves the sides of the pan clean. Cool for a few minutes and then add the eggs, one at a time, beating well after each. The pastry should be just firm enough to hold its shape.

Drop spoonfuls of pastry onto a greased baking sheet. When they are well risen and golden, cool on a wire rack.

To make the filling, combine the sugar, cornflour and flour. Add the lightly beaten egg and yolk. Mix well. Gradually add the scalded milk, stirring constantly. Return to the pan and cook over a low heat, stirring, until thick and smooth. Cool.

To assemble the cream puffs, split the choux buns nearly in half and open slightly. Fill each one with a spoonful of custard and arrange on one large or several individual serving dishes. Sprinkle with sieved icing sugar.

To cook conventionally: Bake the choux buns at 220° for 15 minutes.

To cook in a fan oven: Bake the choux buns at 210° for 15 minutes.

To cook in a multifunction oven: Use the setting for fan + bottom. Bake the choux buns at 210° for 15 minutes.

Variations

Fill the choux buns with whipped cream, chocolate cream or ice cream. Top with chocolate or butterscotch sauce instead of icing sugar.

Pipe the choux pastry onto the baking sheets in finger shapes to make eclairs. Fill with custard or cream and top with chocolate icing.

Arrange spoonfuls of pastry in a ring on the baking tray. After cooling, fill with butter cream flavoured with praline, custard or whipped cream. Top with a caramel icing and decorate with crystallised fruit.

Fill the choux buns with a savoury mixture of vegetables, ham, fish or poultry in a light cream sauce to serve as an hors d'oeuvre or on a buffet.

CAKES AND COOKIES

Poppy Seed Cake

Ingredients	Metric	Imperial	American
Margarine	50 g	2 oz	1/4 cup
Sugar	125 g	4 oz	1/2 cup
Egg	1	1	1
Lemon juice	5 ml	1 tsp	1 tsp
Lemon rind	5 ml	1 tsp	1 tsp
Flour	125 g	4 oz	1 cup
Baking powder	2 1/2 ml	1/2 tsp	1/2 tsp
Baking soda	2 1/2 ml	1/2 tsp	1/2 tsp
Salt	pinch	pinch	pinch
Sour cream	120 ml	4 fl oz	1/2 cup
Raisins	75 g	3 oz	1/2 cup
Poppy seeds	25 ml	5 tsp	5 tsp

Cream the margarine with 75 g/3 oz/1/3 cup sugar until light and fluffy. Add the lightly beaten egg and mix well. Stir in the lemon juice and finely grated rind.

Sieve the flour with the baking powder, soda and salt. Fold into the egg mixture along with the sour cream. Mix well. Add the raisins and 10 ml/2 tsp poppy seeds. Spoon into a greased and lined 20 cm/8 inch square tin or a small ring tin (ring mold). Smooth the top. Sprinkle with the remaining sugar and poppy seeds.

To cook conventionally: Bake for 35 minutes at 175° or until a skewer inserted in the centre comes out clean.
To cook in a fan oven: Bake for 35 minutes at 160° or until a skewer inserted in the centre comes out clean.
To cook in a multifunction oven: Use the setting for fan or conventional cooking only and proceed as above.

Carrot Cake

Ingredients	Metric	Imperial	American
Eggs	4	4	4
Sugar	175 g	6 oz	¾ cup
Grated carrots	225 g	8 oz	1 cup
Ground almonds	225 g	8 oz	½ cup
Flour	50 g	2 oz	½ cup
Baking powder	5 ml	1 tsp	1 tsp
Salt	pinch	pinch	pinch

Whisk the eggs with the sugar until thick and light. Add all the remaining ingredients and mix well. Grease and line a 20 cm/8 inch square cake tin with paper. Pour the batter into the tin and level the top.

Serve the carrot cake as it is or top with either a cream cheese or glacé icing and garnish with toasted almonds. You can also bake the cake in a round pan, 20 cm/8 inches in diameter. When it is cool, cut into two layers and sandwich together with a cream cheese or butter icing.

Sprinkle the top with icing (confectioners') sugar.

To cook conventionally: Bake for 35–40 minutes at 190°.
To cook in a fan oven: Bake for 35 minutes at 180°.
To cook in a multifunction oven: Use the setting for fan or conventional cooking only and proceed as above.

Yoghurt Cake

Ingredients	Metric	Imperial	American
Margarine	125 g	4 oz	½ cup
Sugar	175 g	6 oz	¾ cup
Eggs	3	3	3
Grated lemon rind	5 ml	1 tsp	1 tsp
Natural yoghurt	150 ml	5 fl oz	⅔ cup
Flour	225 g	8 oz	2 cups
Baking powder	15 ml	3 tsp	3 tsp
Salt	pinch	pinch	pinch

Cream the margarine and sugar until light and fluffy. Add the lightly beaten eggs, one at a time, beating well after each. Add the lemon rind and yoghurt. Mix well. Use set or thick Greek yoghurt if you can.

Sieve the flour with the baking powder and salt. Fold into the batter. Turn into a greased and lined 20 cm/8 inch square tin.

To cook conventionally: Bake the Yoghurt Cake for 40 minutes at 180°.

To cook in a fan oven: Bake the Yoghurt Cake for 35 minutes at 160°.

To cook in a multifunction oven: Use the setting for fan or conventional cooking only and proceed as above.

Carrot Cake (p. 112)

Slimmers' Cheesecake

Ingredients	Metric	Imperial	American
Digestive biscuits (graham crackers)	225 g	8 oz	2 cups
Cinnamon	pinch	pinch	pinch
Margarine	50g	2 oz	¼ cup
Cottage cheese	225 g	8 oz	1 cup
Fromage frais	225 g	8 oz	1 cup
Egg	1	1	1
Sugar	125 g	4 oz	½ cup
Lemon	½	½	½
Cornflour (cornstarch)	30 ml	2 tbsp	2 tbsp
Unsalted butter	25 g	1 oz	2 tbsp
Sour cream	150 ml	5 fl oz	⅔ cup
Vanilla essence (extract)	2 ½ ml	½ tsp	½ tsp
Sugar	10 ml	2 tsp	2 tsp

Crush the digestive biscuits to make crumbs and combine with the cinnamon and melted margarine. Press into the base and partially up the sides of a 20 cm/8 inch loose bottomed pan. Any other plain biscuit you like can be used instead of digestives – try morning coffee or afternoon tea for a change.

Sieve the cottage cheese and mix with the fromage frais, egg, sugar, grated rind and juice of the lemon, cornflour and melted butter. Mix well. Pour onto the crumb base. Bake as below.

Whisk the sour cream with the vanilla and sugar. Spread gently over the baked cheesecake and return to the oven.

Cool the cheesecake thoroughly and chill before serving. For extra variation you can also top the cake with pieces of fresh fruit and a light glaze or a fruit purée after it has cooled.

To cook conventionally: Bake the cheesecake for 30 minutes at 170°. Top with sour cream and bake for an additional 15 minutes or until set.

To cook in a fan oven: Bake the cheesecake for 30 minutes at 150°. Top with sour cream and bake for an additional 10 minutes or until set.

To cook in a multifunction oven: Use the setting for fan or conventional cooking only and proceed as above.

Quick Fruit Cake

Ingredients	Metric	Imperial	American
Sugar	175 g	6 oz	¾ cup
Salt	2 ½ ml	½ tsp	½ tsp
Ground cloves	2 ½ ml	½ tsp	½ tsp
Ground cinnamon	2 ½ ml	½ tsp	½ tsp
Ground nutmeg	2 ½ ml	½ tsp	½ tsp
Cocoa	5 ml	1 tsp	1 tsp
Water	225 ml	8 fl oz	1 cup
Raisins	125 g	4 oz	⅔ cup
Vegetable oil	120 ml	4 fl oz	½ cup
Apple	1	1	1
Plain (all-purpose) flour	125 g	4 oz	1 cup
Wholewheat flour	125 g	4 oz	1 cup
Baking soda	15 ml	1 tbsp	1 tbsp
Chopped walnuts	125 g	4 oz	1 cup

Place the sugar, salt, cloves, cinnamon, nutmeg and cocoa in a large pan. Mix well. Add the water, raisins, oil and chopped apple. Bring to the boil, reduce the heat and simmer gently for 5 minutes. Leave to cool until lukewarm.

Combine the plain and wholewheat flours with the baking soda. Fold into the spice mixture. Add the walnuts. Mix well. Turn into a greased and lined 20 cm/8 inch round or square tin.

Serve the cake as it is or top with glacé icing made with either lemon juice or maple syrup and icing (confectioners') sugar. Garnish with walnut halves. If you make a round cake, split in half after cooling to make two layers and sandwich with coffee- or maple-flavoured butter icing.

To cook conventionally: Bake the cake for 35–40 minutes at 180°.
To cook in a fan oven: Bake the cake for 35–40 minutes at 160°.
To cook in a multifunction oven: Use the setting for fan or conventional cooking only and proceed as above.

Many Splendoured Cookies

Ingredients	Metric	Imperial	American
Unsalted butter	125 g	4 oz	½ cup
Sugar	125 g	4 oz	½ cup
Eggs	3	3	3
Vanilla or almond essence (extract) OR	2 ½ ml	½ tsp	½ tsp
Lemon	½	½	½
Plain flour	225–350 g	8–12 oz	2–3 cups
Baking powder	5 ml	1 tsp	1 tsp
Milk	15 ml	1 tbsp	1 tbsp

Cream the butter and sugar until light and fluffy. Add the lightly beaten eggs, one at a time, beating well after each. Stir in the vanilla or almond essence for flavouring, or use the juice and finely grated rind of the lemon.

Sieve the flour with the baking powder. Add to the egg mixture. The amount of flour you use depends on whether you want to make soft, dropping cookies or have a firmer dough for rolling and filling. Stir in the milk to bind the mixture if using the larger amount of flour.

If you are making soft dropping cookies, simply place spoonfuls on greased baking trays, allowing enough space for the cookies to spread while they are baking. If you prefer to roll the cookies to make shapes, add extra flour so that the dough is firm enough to handle. Wrap in clingfilm and chill for 1 hour. Roll the dough to the desired thickness and cut to shape. Alternatively, roll the dough to make one large rectangle, spread with your favourite filling (see right) and roll as for a Swiss roll (jelly roll). Slice thinly and arrange on greased baking trays.

To cook conventionally: Bake the cookies for 8–10 minutes at 180°.

To cook in a fan oven: Bake the cookies for 8–10 minutes at 170°.

To cook in a multifunction oven: Use the setting for fan or conventional cooking only and proceed as above.

Variations

Top dropped cookies with a glacé cherry, almond or walnut or mix pieces of fruit, nuts or chocolate into the batter before placing on the baking trays.

If you have cut the cookies to shape, sandwich two together with jam, lemon curd, butter icing or chocolate. Alternatively, ice the tops or just the edges depending on the shape and sprinkle with chocolate strands, finely chopped nuts or desiccated coconut.

For rolled cookies, spread the dough with a mixture of cinnamon, sugar, nuts and raisins, chocolate, jam or peanut butter mixed with chopped dates.

Cherry Chocolate Cake

Ingredients	Metric	Imperial	American
White wine vinegar	5 ml	1 tsp	1 tsp
Milk	120 ml	4 fl oz	½ cup
Margarine	125 g	4 oz	½ cup
Sugar	175 g	6 oz	¾ cup
Egg	1	1	1
Flour	225 g	8 oz	2 cups
Baking soda	5 ml	1 tsp	1 tsp
Baking powder	10 ml	2 tsp	2 tsp
Salt	pinch	pinch	pinch
Cocoa powder	50 g	2 oz	3 tbsp
Kirsch	50 ml	2 fl oz	¼ cup
Glacé (candied) cherries	50 g	2 oz	¼ cup

Combine the vinegar with enough milk to make 120 ml/4 fl oz/½ cup and leave to stand for 10 minutes or until the milk begins to curdle.

Cream the margarine and sugar until light and fluffy. Add the lightly beaten egg and mix well.

Sieve the flour with the baking soda, baking powder, salt and cocoa. Fold into the egg mixture alternately with the milk and Kirsch, mixing well after each addition. Stir in the chopped cherries.

Spoon the batter into a greased and lined tin and smooth the top. You can use either a 450 g/1 lb loaf tin, a 20 cm/8 inch round or square tin or a 12-hole bun tin.

To cook conventionally: Bake a loaf, round or square cake for 45 minutes at 190°. Bake small cakes for 15–20 minutes.
To cook in a fan oven: Bake a loaf, round or square cake for 45 minutes at 175°. Bake small cakes for 15–20 minutes.
To cook in a multifunction oven: Use the setting for fan or conventional cooking only and proceed as above.

Raisin Cheesecake

Ingredients	Metric	Imperial	American
Digestive biscuits (graham crackers)	125 g	4 oz	1 cup
Sugar	15 ml	1 tbsp	1 tbsp
Ground cinnamon	5 ml	1 tsp	1 tsp
Butter or margarine	45 ml	3 tbsp	3 tbsp
Cottage cheese	225 g	8 oz	1 cup
Curd cheese	225 g	8 oz	1 cup
Eggs, separated	2	2	2
Lemon rind	5 ml	1 tsp	1 tsp
Sugar	50 g	2 oz	1/4 cup
Raisins	50 g	2 oz	1/3 cup
Sultanas (golden raisins)	50 g	2 oz	1/3 cup

Crush the digestive biscuits to make crumbs and combine with the sugar, cinnamon and melted butter. Press into the base and partially up the sides of a 20 cm/8 inch loose-bottomed pan. Any other plain biscuit you like can be used instead of digestives – try morning coffee or afternoon tea for a change.

Sieve the cottage cheese to reduce some of the larger lumps. Beat with the curd cheese until smooth. Add the lightly beaten egg yolks and mix well. Stir in the grated lemon rind, sugar, raisins and sultanas.

Whisk the egg whites until they are stiff but not dry. Gently fold into the cheese mixture, starting with just one spoonful and gradually adding the remainder. Pour onto the biscuit base.

To cook conventionally: Bake at 180° for 30 minutes or until set. Cool the cheesecake in the oven with the door slightly ajar.

To cook in a fan oven: Bake at 160° for 30 minutes or until set. Cool the cheesecake in the oven with the door slightly ajar.

To cook in a multifunction oven: Use the setting for fan or conventional cooking only and proceed as above.

(Illustrated on p. 21)

BREAD AND YEAST COOKING

Coffee-Time Cake

Ingredients	Metric	Imperial	American
Milk	175 ml	6 fl oz	¾ cup
Butter	125 g	4 oz	½ cup
Easy blend yeast	1 pkg	1 pkg	1 pkg
Strong flour	675 g	1 ½ lb	6 cups
Sugar	125 g	4 oz	½ cup
Salt	5 ml	1 tsp	1 tsp
Eggs	3	3	3
Warm water	120 ml	4 fl oz	½ cup

Heat the milk and butter until the butter has melted. Cool to lukewarm.

Combine the yeast, flour, sugar and salt. If you are using ordinary dried yeast or fresh yeast, dissolve in the warm water and leave for 10 minutes or until it begins to bubble.

Add the milk and lightly beaten eggs to the flour and mix to form a dough. Gradually add the water as necessary. Knead the dough until it is firm and elastic. Place in a greased bowl, cover and leave to rise until it has doubled in bulk, approximately 1 hour. If you have a fan or multifunction oven with a setting for defrost, the dough can be placed in the oven, but there must not be any heat.

Punch the dough down, fold to make a ball and cut into thirds. Each piece can be rolled out to make a large square or rectangle and filled with either marzipan mixed with eggs and butter, any combination of fruit and nuts you like, or a cheese filling flavoured with sugar and cinnamon. You can also spread the dough with jam or a fruit purée, plain or flavoured with liqueur.

Seal the dough and shape to make a square, circle or

crescent. Place on a greased baking tray, cover and leave to rise for 1 hour.

Serve the Coffee-Time Cake warm or cold, plain, sprinkled with icing (confectioners') sugar or topped with a glacé icing. Alternatively, shape the dough into a round, leave to rise and then sprinkle with a streusel topping made from flour, butter, sugar and chopped nuts.

To cook conventionally: Bake the cake at 180° for 35–40 minutes or until well risen and golden.
To cook in a fan oven: Bake the cake at 160° for 35–40 minutes or until well risen and golden.
To cook in a multifunction oven: Use the setting for fan or conventional cooking only and proceed as above.

Muffins

Ingredients	Metric	Imperial	American
Flour	225 g	8 oz	2 cups
Baking powder	15 ml	1 tbsp	1 tbsp
Salt	2 ½ ml	½ tsp	½ tsp
Sugar	30 ml	2 tbsp	2 tbsp
Melted butter	50 g	2 oz	¼ cup
Egg	1	1	1
Milk	225 ml	8 fl oz	1 cup

Sieve the flour and mix with the baking powder, salt and sugar. You can use plain (all-purpose) flour, wholewheat or a combination. Cornmeal or porridge oats can also be substituted for half of the flour.

Stir the melted butter into the lightly beaten egg. Add the milk and mix well. Pour over the flour and mix until just blended. Spoon into greased bun tins.

To cook conventionally: Bake the muffins for 15–20 minutes at 200°.
To cook in a fan oven: Bake the muffins for 15–20 minutes at 180°.
To cook in a multifunction oven: Use the setting for fan or conventional cooking only and proceed as above.

Variations

Add fresh, frozen or dried fruit to the flour before adding the liquid ingredients. Try berries of any sort, diced apples, dates, sultanas (golden raisins), etc.

Add cinnamon, nutmeg, ground ginger or mixed spice to taste.

If you are using cornmeal, substitute bacon fat for part of the melted butter and stir in a few spoonfuls of sweetcorn.

After baking the muffins, sprinkle them with sugar mixed with grated orange or lemon rind, cinnamon or mixed spice or brown sugar mixed with chopped nuts. The latter can be popped under the grill (broiler) for 2–3 minutes to caramelise.

To make savoury muffins, flavour the batter with grated cheese, dried mustard and/or crispy bacon.

Sourdough Bread

Ingredients	Metric	Imperial	American
Starter			
Dried yeast	5 ml	1 tsp	1 tsp
Strong flour	225 g	8 oz	2 cups
Milk	450 ml	¾ pint	2 cups
Sugar	125 g	4 oz	½ cup
Bread			
Milk	225 ml	8 fl oz	1 cup
Margarine	30 ml	1 oz	2 tbsp
Strong flour	675 g	1 ½ lb	6 cups
Sugar	15 ml	1 tbsp	1 tbsp
Salt	5 ml	1 tsp	1 tsp
Easy blend yeast	1 pkg	1 pkg	1 pkg
Starter	350 ml	12 fl oz	1 ½ cups

The sourdough starter needs 3–4 days to mature, but once started, can be topped up and kept indefinitely. Combine the dried yeast with half each of the flour, milk and sugar. Keep in an uncovered bowl in the kitchen and stir down two or three times a day. The remaining flour, milk and sugar should be added 8 hours before you are ready to use the starter.

To make Sourdough Bread, heat the milk with the

margarine until the margarine has melted. Cool until it is lukewarm.

Combine the flour, sugar, salt and yeast. If you are using ordinary dried or fresh yeast, mix with some of the lukewarm milk and leave for 10 minutes or until it is bubbly.

Add the milk and starter to the flour. Mix to make a stiff dough and knead until firm and elastic. Place in a greased bowl, cover and leave to rise until it has doubled in bulk, approximately 1 hour in a warm place. If your oven has a defrost programme, you can use it provided there is no heat being circulated.

Punch down the dough, shape to fit into a loaf tin, cover and leave to rise again.

To cook conventionally: Bake the Sourdough Bread for 20–30 minutes at 200°.

To cook in a fan oven: Bake the Sourdough Bread for 20–30 minutes at 190°.

To cook in a multifunction oven: Use the setting for fan or conventional cooking only and proceed as above.

Variation
Substitute wholewheat or rye flour for half of the strong white flour when mixing the bread dough.

To make Sourdough Biscuits, use 225 ml/8 fl oz/1 cup starter to bind your favourite scone (biscuit) mixture. Knead well, cut to shape and leave to rise for 30 minutes. Bake for 10–15 minutes at 210° in a conventional oven or 200° in a fan or multifunction oven.

Dinner Rolls

Ingredients	Metric	Imperial	American
Milk	225 ml	8 fl oz	1 cup
Butter	30 ml	2 tbsp	2 tbsp
Easy blend yeast	5 ml	1 tsp	1 tsp
Strong flour	350 g	12 oz	3 cups
Sugar	15 ml	1 tbsp	1 tbsp
Salt	2 ½ ml	½ tsp	½ tsp
Egg (optional)	1	1	1

Warm the milk with the butter until the butter has melted. Leave to cool until it is lukewarm.

Combine the yeast, flour, sugar and salt. If you are using ordinary dried or fresh yeast, dissolve in the warm milk and leave for 10 minutes or until bubbly. Stir in the flour mixture and mix to form a stiff dough. Knead well, place in a clean bowl and cover. Leave to rise until double in bulk, approximately 1 hour. Alternatively, for no-knead rolls, use 250 g/8 oz/2 cups flour. Add the beaten egg with the milk and mix well to make a batter. Cover and leave to rise for 1 hour or until the surface is very bubbly.

Punch or stir down the mixture. If you are using dough, cut into 12 pieces and shape to make the rolls. Arrange on a greased baking tray. If you are using batter, spoon into greased bun tins, leaving each one only half full. Cover the rolls and leave to rise in a warm place for 30 minutes.

To cook conventionally: Bake for 15 minutes at 200°.
To cook in a fan oven: Bake for 15 minutes at 180°.
To cook in a multifunction oven: Use the setting for fan only.

Pizza

Ingredients	Metric	Imperial	American
Easy blend yeast	1 pkg	1 pkg	1 pkg
Strong flour	675 g	1 ½ lb	6 cups
Salt	10 ml	2 tsp	2 tsp

Boiling water	150 ml	5 fl oz	⅔ cup
Cold water	300 ml	½ pt	1 ¼ cups
Olive oil	30 ml	2 tbsp	2 tbsp

Combine the yeast, flour and salt. If you are using ordinary dried yeast or fresh yeast, dissolve in warm water and leave for 10 minutes or until it begins to bubble.

Combine the hot and cold water. Stir the olive oil into the flour and gradually add the water as necessary. Knead the dough until it is firm and elastic. Place in a greased bowl, cover and leave to rise until it has doubled in bulk, approximately 1 hour. If you have a fan or multifunction oven with a setting for defrost, the dough can be placed in the oven, but there must not be any heat.

Punch the dough down and knead once more to make a smooth ball. Cut into as many pieces as you plan to make

pizzas. Roll out to make thin discs which just fit your tins, leaving the edges a little bit thicker than the centre to hold the filling. Cover and leave to rise for 15 minutes.

Top the pizza with the fillings of your choice: a well flavoured tomato sauce, grated Mozzarella cheese, olives, mushrooms, salami, courgettes (zucchini), onions, chillis, peppers etc. and fresh herbs as available. Top with a sprinkling of grated cheese and drizzle with a few drops of olive oil.

To cook conventionally: Bake the pizza at 225° for 15–20 minutes according to size. The cheese should be melted and the crust well risen and golden at the edges.

To cook in a fan oven: Bake the pizza at 210° for 15–20 minutes according to size. The cheese should be melted and the crust well risen and golden at the edges.

To cook in a multifunction oven: Use the setting for fan + bottom. Bake the pizza at 210° for 15–20 minutes according to size. The cheese should be melted and the crust well risen and golden at the edges.

Cheese Twist

Ingredients	Metric	Imperial	American
Milk	175 ml	6 fl oz	¾ cup
Butter	30 ml	1 oz	2 tbsp
Easy blend yeast	1 pkg	1 pkg	1 pkg
Strong flour	675 g	1 ½ lb	6 cups
Salt	5 ml	1 tsp	1 tsp
Dry mustard (optional)	5 ml	1 tsp	1 tsp
Warm water	225 ml	8 oz	1 cup
Grated Cheddar cheese	125 g	4 oz	1 cup
Onion or celery (optional)	50 g	2 oz	½ cup
Egg	1	1	1
Sesame or poppy seeds	15 ml	1 tbsp	1 tbsp

Heat the milk and butter until the butter has melted. Cool to lukewarm.

Combine the yeast, flour, salt and mustard. If you are using ordinary dried yeast or fresh yeast, dissolve in the warm water and leave for 10 minutes or until it begins to bubble.

Stir the grated cheese and finely chopped onion or celery into the flour. Add the milk and butter and mix to form a dough. Gradually add the water as necessary. Knead the dough until it is firm and elastic. Place in a greased bowl, cover and leave to rise until it has doubled in bulk, approximately 1 hour. If you have a fan or multifunction oven with a setting for defrost, the dough can be placed in the oven, but there must not be any heat.

Punch down the dough and divide into three pieces. Roll each one with your hands to make strips approximately 25–30 cm/10–12 inches long. Place the strips side by side. Pinch together at the end furthest from you. Cross the strip on your left over the one in the centre. Cross the strip on your right over the one which is now in the centre. Repeat this process, crossing first from the left, then from the right, until you have reached the end. Pinch together. Gently lift onto a greased baking sheet, cover and leave to rise in a warm place for 1 hour. Brush with lightly beaten egg and sprinkle with seeds.

To cook conventionally: Bake at 200° for 25–30 minutes or until well risen and golden. The bread should sound hollow when tapped on its bottom.
To cook in a fan oven: Bake at 180° for 25–30 minutes or until well risen and golden. The bread should sound hollow when tapped on its bottom.
To cook in a multifunction oven: Use the setting for fan or conventional cooking only and proceed as above.

Index